WORKING WITH PEOPLE
IN COMMUNITY ACTION

Working with People

FOR TRAINED COMMUNITY

in Community Action

AN INTERNATIONAL CASEBOOK

WORKERS AND VOLUNTEER

COMMUNITY LEADERS

by Clarence King, PROFESSOR EMERITUS,
NEW YORK SCHOOL OF SOCIAL WORK, COLUMBIA
UNIVERSITY · CONSULTANT ON COMMUNITY
DEVELOPMENT, UNITED NATIONS, 1952–1955

ASSOCIATION PRESS

Publisher's stock number: 1591
Library of Congress catalog card number: 65–21965

Printed in the United States of America

"Put love first; but there are other gifts of the Spirit at which you should aim also, and above all prophecy. . . . When a man prophesies, he is talking to men, and his words have power to build; they stimulate and they encourage. The language of ecstasy is good for the speaker himself, but it is prophecy that builds up a community. . . . The prophet is worth more than the man of ecstatic speech—unless indeed he can explain its meaning, and so help to build up the community."

(I Corinthians 14:1-6, in part—*The New English Bible*)

CONTENTS

on a national scale? (*Vocational Rehabilitation in Israel*) . . .
How widely applicable are the principles we have been discussing? (*Kilworth, Ireland; Kitoi, Kenya*).

WORKING WITH PEOPLE
IN COMMUNITY ACTION

I. INTRODUCTORY

What is "community action"?

In 1830 Alexis de Tocqueville visited the United States. In amazement he wrote back to France:

These Americans are the most peculiar people in the world. You'll not believe it when I tell you how they behave. In a local community in their country a citizen may conceive of some need which is not being met. What does he do? He goes across the street and discusses it with his neighbor. Then what happens? A committee comes into existence and then the committee begins functioning on behalf of that need and you won't believe this but it's true. All of this is done without reference to any bureaucrat. All of this is done by private citizens on their own initiative.

Such committee work is the simplest form of "community action." But in this book we shall include under this term all efforts conducted in newly developing countries throughout the world under the term "community development" (see the Appendix, "Concerning Definitions"), provided the ultimate purpose of such efforts is to build a stronger community and more self-reliant citizens as well as to provide a better highway or canal, or to provide electric power, or whatever is needed.

We shall also include as community action what social workers call "community organization." This includes forming and operating a neighborhood council, a community council, or a united community fund. It also covers bringing into being a local social agency and all efforts to stimulate citizen interest, co-operation, and support of health, welfare, or educational services whether under unofficial or government auspices.

We shall exclude from this book all action taken directly by national or local governments through their salaried representatives unless the voluntary efforts of local citizens are intimately involved.

In a discussion of community development at the United Nations a delegate stated that such efforts to stimulate self-help were praiseworthy but that "they would not be necessary if the government did what it should for its citizens." We who believe in what we call democracy would disagree with this delegate. We decry government paternalism. Believing in "government by the consent of the governed" and "of the people, by the people, for the people," we would stimulate voluntary citizen action. Hence we would exalt just such community action as amazed de Tocqueville.

The term "community action" has recently come into official use through the passage of the Economic Opportunity Act. This is the so-called Antipoverty Bill signed by the President, August 20, 1964. Title II of the Act authorizes the Director of the Office of Economic Opportunity to enter into agreements with public or private nonprofit agencies to assist them with the cost of developing *"community action* programs."

Why a "case book"?

The process of stimulating and organizing a community for action is older than history and has been practiced in many nations. Moses was adept at it, and so was Gandhi. It is a difficult art. No one has yet deduced from it a dependable set of scientific principles which can be taught by lectures or memorized from books. It must be learned by doing. Those most proficient in it have never stopped to record and analyze how they got their results. They have worked intuitively and probably could not explain exactly why or how they have proceeded.

I have recently seen at the United Nations an attempted list of the "social skills" that are needed by a community worker. The memorandum said: "In the present state of our knowledge any check list that sets out to cover them is little more than empirical and no claim is made that they can be related to specific scientific concepts or taught in conjunction with them." Then followed a list of forty-six items. The first three are listed here as a sample:

(1) How to approach a . . . community so as to win its confidence.
(2) How to find out significant facts about the . . . community without house-to-house inquiries.
(3) How to recognize local leaders and the bases of their leadership.

In an effort to answer "how they [these social skills] may best be acquired or developed" the memorandum then quoted from an evaluation made by a committee consisting of Dr. Margaret Read and others as to a "syllabus carefully drawn up by expert committees at New Delhi to guide and delimit the community development courses." Dr. Read's committee questioned whether theoretical lectures based on such a syllabus were not a waste of time and money; and she suggested that at least "an appendix should be attached to each syllabus containing actual problems which arise in a village context, relating to village organization, the emergence of new leaders, et cetera. . . . Such examples should be drawn from real life situations and not invented by someone remote from village realities."

In preparing this case book, I have sought to gather such realistic "examples" and "actual problems" and to deduce therefrom certain lessons which might help community workers in dealing with people in various communities here and abroad. Of some sixty-two such cases or examples stated or mentioned in this book, most of them came from the files of the United Nations or the U.S. International Co-operation Administration (ICA), supplemented by my own experience of forty years of working with people in many communities large and small.

For whom is this book intended?

A. In newly developing communities, particularly in Asia, Africa, and Latin America:

    (1) for village-level workers or front-line development workers (if they can read English),

    (2) for those who train and supervise them, and

    (3) for volunteer community leaders who work with them.

B. In urban and other more sophisticated communities on whatever continent:

    (1) for the volunteer leaders of such communities,

    (2) for executives of neighborhood or community councils,

    (3) for social workers engaged in community organization or community development, and

    (4) for students training for community organization or community development.

To be fully useful it should meet the needs of a village-level worker in India, of a field-group organizer in Puerto Rico, of an agricultural extension agent among the Indian farmers of New Mexico, or of the volunteer chairman of a neighborhood council in Newark, New Jersey.

May the book be at hand to reassure a community worker when he is tempted to lose his faith in the ability of his community to help itself. May it preach patience when he is urged to win an immediate victory by methods which will defeat his ultimate purpose, namely, to build a stronger community of more self-reliant individuals. May it be at hand when he must choose between two or more difficult courses of action. It will not answer his specific problem, but it may stimulate deeper thought resulting in a wise decision.

Why is community action emergently important in the 1960's?

On a Sunday morning a small boy had been cautioned by his parents to let them sleep. When the clock struck eight it proved out of order and went on striking nine, ten, eleven, twelve, and still it could not stop. The boy rushed upstairs crying, "Father, Mother, wake up! It's later than it's *ever* been before!"

Today there is an imperative need for community action for it is "later than it's ever been before." For example: In the 1890's an immigrant youth, named Jacob Riis, came to the United States from Denmark. He became a police reporter on the lower East Side of New York. He was shocked by the deplorable conditions in the tenements. He wrote a book called *How the Other Half Lives*. This came into the hands of the vigorous young police commissioner, Theodore Roosevelt. Together the two young men tramped the filthy stairs of the East Side. "Teddy" acquired a social vision which stood him in good stead when he became President. But community conscience was slow to rouse. At last by 1950 these old tenements were pulled down and "Jacob Riis Houses"—model apartments—now stand in their stead.

Today we in the United States cannot afford to wait fifty years to tackle "this unfinished business of Democracy." The world has shrunk, and the eyes of millions are upon us. We prate of equality of opportunity. If today one individual among us is deprived of his rights as a citizen, tomorrow it is news in the capitals of Europe, Asia, and Africa; and this is used abroad to prove that democracy is too slow a process.

In the next ten years millions of people will make a world-shaking decision: between those who preach the supposed efficiency of police state discipline and those of us who believe that real efficiency comes with freedom of the spirit. The war is not primarily one between ideologies. All men are arrayed against the three allies—hunger, ignorance, and disease—but our army is divided. One camp would win by rigid control from above, subordinating the individual and his community. The other would build from the bottom, dignifying the individual and strengthening the local community and through it the nation and the world. In the end the issue will be decided not by the bomb but by those who stimulate and lead communities to action, by each of us wherever we may live, by good citizenship in our own hometown. From this standpoint, when Mr. Shahrifzadeh in Iran (see the story of Galino, Iran, in Chapter IV) led four hundred of his neighbors to construct a good school building by their own efforts he was serving not only the village of Galino: he was serving us as well and all who love freedom and the democratic way of life.

*   *   *

Summary. Community action embraces both community development and community organization. Its main purpose is to build a stronger community for the future. It is an art best taught by doing or by group discussion of realistic case material. It is vastly important in the 1960's if the democratic way of life is to survive.

II. GETTING
ACQUAINTED

In this chapter let us see what case materials we can assemble which will help us to answer the three problems quoted in Chapter I from the United Nations list of "Social Skills" needed by a community worker.

How to approach a community so as to win its confidence

Suh Kam Chon, Korea

In 1953 Glen Leet was head of a small staff in the United Nations secretariat specializing in Community Development for underdeveloped countries. In the years following the war he had been sent by the United Nations to assist the Greek Government. He succeeded in stimulating some 1500 Greek villages to self-help efforts to improve their roads, drain marshes, install water supply systems, etc., etc.—all by harnessing the voluntary efforts of unemployed villagers who worked for the benefits to their town rather than for a few cents a day awarded by the Greek Government as an honorary bonus for those who took part.

19

In March 1953 Leet went to Korea to discover whether a similar plan could help to solve some of the rural problems of the Republic of Korea. He visited the village of Suh Kam Chon, some ten miles from Pusan. The first person interviewed was an ordinary workman who was treading mud and straw together for plastering a house. Recognizing that he had a sympathetic listener, the man talked freely. He said that the period of fullest employment in Suh Kam Chon was from May through July. There was a relatively dead season in August and September. During October and November the villagers were engaged in harvesting and in collecting firewood. During the period of December through April, there was little work although some of the villagers got employment in Pusan. The laborer interviewed was employed for one week and sometimes two weeks during the month. He was paid 100 Hwan.* During the year if he was lucky he worked for seven months; if he was not so lucky, he was likely to have six months' employment.

Soon another man stopped by and joined the group. Both said that the greatest need of the village was to deepen an irrigation canal. At this point they were joined by the Ku Chang [village president]. He concurred with the opinions expressed by the others that the urgent need of the community was the improvement of their canal system. He said it would give them a better control of water and would increase production in that area of eighty chumbos† from 150 suks‡ to 250 suks. The value of this additional 100 suks would be 600,000 Hw, he said. The project would require 300 man-days of work, he estimated. When the villagers, who now had gathered about, realized the great benefit which would result from the work, their enthusiasm was greatly increased.

The prevailing rate in that village for agricultural labor was 100 Hw per day plus free meals. The villagers agreed, however, that they should not expect that compensation when they were working on something which would benefit them so greatly. They said that the persons who benefited from this would be willing to work for 25 Hw a day. In this village of 140 families there were 100 workers. This low

* The official rate was 60 Hw to the dollar, and the free market rate was 250 Hw to the dollar.
† A chumbo is about 2.5 acres.
‡ A suk of unpolished rice is about ½ of a metric ton.

figure was accounted for by the fact that so many of the young people were serving in the army. Underemployment throughout the year was estimated at 35 per cent or 10,500 man-hours annually. (This could be a substantial asset to the community if it could be employed to improve the village.)

Glen Leet was resolved under no circumstances to try to sell any idea or to try to persuade the villagers to undertake any action. The villagers were encouraged to explain their plans in detail and were asked to indicate specifically who would benefit and to what degree. It was Leet's experience that they were generally persuaded by their own arguments, but would react negatively if outsiders made an effort to influence them. He had found this to be the basic attitude of farmers to external authority and external ideas in most underdeveloped rural areas.

If villagers demonstrated that they wanted the improvement and were successful in proving that the project would be of great benefit to the community, the idea was praised and the authors were congratulated. (This he did in Suh Kam Chon. Otherwise he would have passed on to some other community.)

Then the following points were discussed:

(a) Whether or not communities could accomplish such things was essentially a question of the "spirit of the people."

(b) The government could not pay people to work for themselves and for their own community as they would be paid if they were working for some other community, or for the government itself.

(c) However good the spirit of the village, it was difficult for the people to work long enough to do a big project unless they received some money because even though the work was done in idle time, it is well known that a working man needs more food than one who is not working.

(d) The government so valued the spirit of the man who would freely and voluntarily offer his time for the good of the community, that it was offering a bonus to all such people as a symbol that their spirit was appreciated. (The people of Suh Kam Chon themselves fixed twenty-five Hwan a day as a bonus.

This was about ten cents, approximately a tenth of a day's wage. This was high enough to cover the cost of the added food a man needed when working, but low enough so that anyone would understand that he was truly volunteering and not working for pay.)

Some villagers insisted that the spirit of their village was so good that everyone wanted to work and did not care whether they received a bonus or not. Leet said that he was opposed to 100 per cent participation. Only those who believed that they would directly benefit should work. Participation must be voluntary. Otherwise the spirit would be lacking. He recognized that the people of spirit would be willing to work for nothing, but this could not be accepted because, as some would be working and others not working, it was only fair that those who worked receive something in recognition of their spirit.

This convinced those with any lingering doubt that they had no ground for objection. There is a latent fear of "voluntary work" as the workers know from experience that whenever there is 100 per cent participation there is at least some social pressure and therefore, such work is not completely voluntary.

As it appeared that the villagers were sincere in their statements that they wanted to participate and as the plan was a simple one which could be accomplished easily, an agreement was drawn up on the spot.

The villagers recorded in a sentence or two what they intended to do; they indicated their estimates of benefits, the number of people who would benefit and those who wished to participate. They estimated the number of days of work required. The village president signed for the village under the statement:

"Nothing is requested except the bonus payment. It is understood that these payments are not a wage but a bonus given in appreciation of the initiative and patriotism of those who freely and voluntarily offer their services for the benefit of their community. Funds received will be used only for bonus payments at twenty-five Hwan per person for each day worked. A record signed by the recipient will be kept and will be open for inspection for anyone, as it will constitute an honor roll of those who worked for their country."

This statement was a vital element. It established a climate of dignity and self-respect. It created a situation where those who participated enjoyed the respect and approval of their friends and neighbors. This being recognized, the bonus was a pleasant reward and it furnished a reason for a project agreement approved by the government.

The project agreement had important psychological implications. The villagers' own idea acquired dignity by being put on paper. It acquired additional dignity when given a project number and still more when the official seal and the signature of the government official who accompanied Leet indicated that it had the approval of the governor. A copy of this was kept by the village and shown with pride to visitors, who came from miles around to see it.

The official who accompanied Leet made a small advance payment (approximately $5) as an evidence of good faith. The fact that such an advance was purely symbolic seemed not to diminish the impact of the story that spread over an entire province in a few days, and Leet went on to other villages where similar results occurred.

Korean officials were committed to the view that the spirit of the program was even more important than its accomplishments, and that this program afforded an opportunity to show every village the difference between a free and democratic government of their own and one of foreign domination. The foreign power had told them what they must do, but their own government asked them what they wanted to do and encouraged them. Provincial officials were warned that any compulsion would spoil this high purpose and that such an attempt would result only in sullen behavior on the part of the workers.

Some of the work undertaken would have been of more lasting value if the villagers had been supplied with cement or other materials. However, offers of supplies would have diffused the psychological impact and would start people thinking about what they could get from the government instead of what they could do for themselves. Such offers also caused delay, because promises that could not be kept immediately were a deterrent to local initiative.

The next morning after Mr. Leet's visit to Suh Kam Chon forty men started work and in two days the irrigation canal was deepened by 200 meters. This was in March, 1953. The word spread throughout the country. By the end of April work had been started in every province.

By the first of December, 1953, 150 projects had been completed and 39 more were underway.[1]

Dean Rusk, U.S. Secretary of State, has been quoted as saying: "One of the best ways to persuade others is with your ears—by listening to them." This seems to have been Glen Leet's technique in Korea. How few of us are good listeners, particularly if we regard ourselves as experts, accustomed to tell others rather than let them tell us. His passive attitude encouraged the villagers to express themselves and to *convince themselves* of the desirability of doing what they themselves had suggested. Leet even raised possible objections to the practicability of their plans. Whereupon *they* showed *him* that it could be done.

Their confidence in him was increased when he arranged to have a small advance payment deposited with the village committee before any work had been done. He trusted the villagers and left the money with them with no safeguards other than faith in the intrinsic honesty of human beings when temptation is overcome by loyalty to their community and enthusiastic interest in an inspiring enterprise. This trust was not foolish sentimentality but wise technique. One is reminded of the classic statement of Secretary of War Stimson to President Truman, in 1945:

The chief lesson I have learned in a long life is that the only way you can make a man trustworthy is to trust him; and the surest way to make a man untrustworthy is to distrust him, and show him your distrust.[2]

When Glen Leet returned to New York from Korea, his colleagues at the United Nations held a staff conference with him. Here is a copy of the notes I took that day headed: "Lessons to be learned from Leet's experience in Korea."

1. Low-powered salesmanship—don't oversell—ask questions—let them convince you—act skeptical and get them to overcome your doubts—let them make it *theirs*.

2. Learn what not to do—more important than what to do—don't be overactive.
3. Villagers know what they want to do for their village—slight incentive (honorary bonus) overcomes inertia.
4. Motivation includes loyalty to village-honor of being included in public honor roll—dignity of taking part in officially approved plan —self-interest and benefit to village—pleasure of being active at something when long unemployed.
5. Make it clear that you can furnish little—no equipment—only small appropriation.

One authority on community development disagrees with Leet as to the wisdom of the honorary bonus and another states that in his country he would not be allowed to trust the villagers with a small deposit. The auditing department would object.

Sarbandan, Iran

[Najmeh Najafi was a young woman of a well-to-do family in Teheran. After studying in America and writing a book *Persia Is My Heart* (in collaboration with Helen Hinckley) which brought her a modest income, she returned to Teheran determined to help the villagers of her native Persia to a better existence within the pattern of their ancient culture. The Ford Foundation granted her a small scholarship with complete independence of action. Here is her own account of how she gained the confidence of the village of Sarbandan where she decided to live and work:]

I clambered out of the ancient automobile which had brought me fifty-six miles from Teheran. . . . I looked over the rooftops of the village to the apricot and cherry orchards fanning up over the foothills; my eyes followed the clear stream of mountain water which we Persians call the jube as it flowed through the center of the village. Along this stream I could see people going and coming. My people. My heart shook for a moment! Perhaps, I thought, perhaps this is the place.

Very near, there was a teahouse. . . . In a moment the owner stood before me. "I would like tea," I told him. "Bring one for yourself too so that we may talk together." As we drank tea he told me that he was

called Mash'hadi Mokhtar and that he was the owner of the place.
. . . "You own a very fine teahouse. But who owns the village?"

"Many own land here."

"No landlords?"

"Some landlords. A few big ones. I am one of these."

"You are a man of importance," I told him.

The man had taken my sincere words for dangerous flattery. Again
his eyes were veiled. "Another tea, my lady?"

"Another tea. A tea for each of us, please." Again he came with the
tea. I curtained my eyes, too, and we were strangers.

"Well, Mashdi Mokhtar, what about the population of Sarbandan?"

"Almost two thousand—in the summer."

"And in the winter?" . . .

"They do not stay in this place . . . they work in the rice fields of
Mazandaran. Only women and children and old men are left here."

We talked for a time and I asked if the people had a bath.

"Bath? How could we have? Our forefathers made one about a
hundred years ago but it is ruined now. Its pool is so unclean that no
one has the desire to go into it." Then he looked at me with a flash of
anger. "My lady, why do you ask these questions of me? Why?"

At this moment I loved Mash'hadi Mokhtar. I loved him because I
saw the fear leap in his eyes, and I understood this fear. My people are
proud and they have much to be proud of. How can they be happy
when so many want to change them?

"Because I think I may want to make my home here, Mashdi
Mokhtar," I said very quietly. "I think perhaps Sarbandan is the place
for us."

He left me and returned with his clopogh, a sort of long pipe. He
drew on it two or three times, then wiping the mouthpiece first with his
fingers then against his cheek, he handed it to me. I drew two or three
suffocating breaths and returned it to him.

"Do you have a school, Mashdi Mokhtar?"

He smiled. Again the gold in his teeth glittered. "Indeed we do. Four
years ago we built the school. We turned it over to the Ministry of
Education. We have grades one, two, three, and four. Next year,
perhaps, we will have five and six. If not next year, at least some
year."

"And is there a school for the girls?"

"What are you talking about, my lady? A school for girls?"

I changed the subject. "Tell me, does Sarbandan have a clinic?"

"Clinic? What is a clinic?"

"A place for care of the sick."

"How could we have such a place when we have no doctor?"

Again there was anger in his voice.

"I am hungry, Mashdi Mokhtar. What can we eat?"

. . . . .

I was glad that Sarbandan was owned by many small landholders and several landlords, because I thought that co-operation would be more easily achieved.

. . . . .

I wanted to work "heart to heart," not in the mechanized way that I had found organizations must move. Besides, I did not want to make a little America in the mountains of Persia. I wanted my people to stay as they were, keeping the feeling of security that goes with doing things the sweet, almost sacred way. I wanted to see if a better way of life could be built on a foundation of native customs and mores. For my people I wanted happiness rather than that colder goal that is sometimes called *progress*.

When Mash'hadi Mokhtar returned . . . I asked, "Do you have a village council?"

"Yes, we have. But the members seldom see each other. When they meet there is nothing but quarreling at the teahouse."

"Tell me, why do the old men quarrel?"

"My lady, in Sarbandan the people are divided into two factions. We even have two Kadkhodas."

"Two Kadkhodas?" A Kadkhoda is a responsible man selected by the large landholders to keep order in the village. . . . "Two Kadkhodas? That is incredible."

"But we have. You see, we are two tribes and our landholders. . . ."

The walls of clinic and school which I had just built in my mind crumbled away. Two factions. Two tribes. Co-operation, which is always hard to achieve with people as individualistic as my people might be impossible. I would have to spend time and energy avoiding petty jealousies, ironing out petty disputes. I could not afford to waste myself that way. I was defeated before I began.

"Come," he said, standing. "Allow me to show you the village, my lady."

Half reluctantly I followed him along the banks of the jube. Women were washing clothes along both sides. The crying of a lamb drew my eyes upstream. Two men were killing the little creature, and its blood was flowing into the water. Between the lamb and the women bent over their washing, a half-grown girl dipped a jug into the stream and lifted it dripping to her shoulders.

Sarbandan needs me, I thought. I looked at the faces of the women and the children. Their skin was transparent; their cheeks like spring petals. Again my heart shook me.

· · · · ·

Four days after my visit to Sarbandan I got up early and took my knapsack and lunch with me. I went to Fouzieh Square and waited until I found a charcoal truck that was going north on the old Mazandaran Road. The driver was not unwilling to have a passenger, so I climbed up in the cab beside him.

· · · · ·

When I went into the teahouse of Mash'hadi Mokhtar [a] boy who had first spoken to me on my other visit came quietly toward me.

"Where is my friend Mashdi Mokhtar? I wish to see him." The boy's face was impassive, but his eyes were friendly. I thought Mashdi Mokhtar had spoken of me to the others.

"Today he is not here. Another day perhaps."

My body ached from the springless drive in the charcoal cart.

"Some other day will not do. Is there a center in the village of Sarbandan?"

"Yes," he said and going out to the road beside me, he pointed the way.

For a time I stood alone in the center of the village.

There were three or four little shops—a shoe-repair place, a barber shop, a house that stocked a few grocery staples—beside the life-giving jube. Some women and children looked at me curiously and hurried away. Finally some old men appeared urging each other forward and asked me what I wanted of them. Evidently Mash'hadi Mokhtar's brother had sent them to me.

There is nothing to be gained by moving too slowly, I thought, so I said boldly, "I have come to start a girls' school in Sarbandan. That is, if you want me to."

"Are you Point Four?"

"No."

The men talked together, then the same spokesman came forward again.

"Are you from Ministry of Education?"

"Nobody sent me here. I came myself. I will live in Sarbandan and teach the school if you wish me to." The spokesman withdrew again, and there was muttering among the men.

"If you have a village council you could discuss a school in your council meeting, then tell me what you decide." This way they will either unite in favor of a school or against it, I thought. In any case they will unite.

The old man came forward again. "We do not see any harm in your proposal," he said. Then a sharp light flickered in his eyes and his voice changed. "Since you are going to live in Sarbandan you will need to find rooms," he suggested, and I thought his eyes turned toward my purse.

. . . . .

I had promised the old men I would be back in a week to select the room which everybody wanted to rent to me and no one wanted to give me for the school. When my friends began to plan an out-of-town picnic I suggested, "Why not some place along the old Mazandaran Road?" . . . "We will all go to Sarbandan," somebody shouted. . . . "No, really," I said. "That would spoil everything." I did not want the village people to think of me as belonging to the city. I must come from nowhere into the village. Almost as if God sent me. That way I would seem to belong to them and that was necessary. So my friend Forough Farschi drove me to Sarbandan.

. . . . .

In Sarbandan the villagers were waiting for me. They took me immediately to the home of the chief of the council. . . . "Let me talk with the householders who showed me the rooms last week."

. . . .

Words of praise about their rooms gave way to quarreling, personal recriminations. But I knew why, and I was not angry. I knew that my presence in a home, my pitifully small rent, would mean the difference between food and hunger for an entire family. These men would be ashamed to face their wives and children if they did not at least put up a good battle. . . .

So we waited until the men had talked themselves out. Then I talked with them, one by one, telling them that the good I would bring to Sarbandan would not rest only under the roof that covered me, but would spread like the morning mist to everyone. Finally I rented a house and contracted to have it gypsum-plastered during the next week. When I asked them to shake hands, kiss, and be happy, they did so, some still muttering in their black mustaches. . . .

"Najmeh," Forough said, "this will be too much for you. You will see. Why should you fight with these people when others would reach out toward your hand?"

I would not let myself think of fighting with these people. People were not my enemies. My enemies were ignorance, greed, superstition, fear, mostly fear. "Some day these people will love and trust me, you will see."

· · · · ·

Nearly all day I worked on the restroom, then in a basin of water from the jube, I cleansed myself for prayer. Shortly after dusk I set out the things for supper: tea, rice, cheese, sugar. In the villages a cone of sugar, harder than the cubes in the American market, and perhaps eighteen inches high and nine in diameter at its base, is considered the most desirable possession in the world. . . .

Three women, wrapped in their chadors, each carrying a lantern, were coming to call on me. They stood outside the doorway until I said, "Won't you come in and have tea with me?" Glancing covertly about them, they came in and stood awkwardly just inside my house. "I am breaking sugar," I told them, not because they could not see me do it but because I must say something and could not speak the questions that were in my head. *Who are you? What names do you have? Are your children healthy? Why do you not keep them clean? How much money do you have for food in a year? Why does no one in the neighborhood ever use a restroom?*

I thought of some of the . . . [agency] social workers asking people who were almost starving for a handful of rice if they were serving their families the seven basic foods every day.

So I might have asked, *What do you know about nutrition?* I could ask none of these questions. Some would never be answered. Some would be answered later—much later.

I said, "I am breaking sugar."

"May I help?" the youngest of the three, a woman of about thirty, asked.

"I would be so grateful. Now I can prepare the tea." I turned the cone over to her.

. . . . .

Many times I have knelt in a mosque at the closing month of Ramazan; but never in a simple mosque like this. . . . And now it is time for each to make quietly his own prayer. . . . I had been asking it in my heart for a long time. "God, give me wisdom and strength and maybe enough money to carry out my work. But above all give me understanding."

After the service I stood in the doorway with a reed basket filled with halva which I offered to the women as they left. . . . I heard one of them say as she turned away from me. "She's young but she is a good Moslem."

I now belonged to Sarbandan.

The next day . . . I began to study my village. I walked through it, sometimes stopping beside the jube to visit with the women who were washing their clothes or their dishes, sometimes stopping at a doorway to speak to a woman making food for her family or caring for her children. The dirt was depressing. . . .

One week passed, and every evening I gave tea to the women who called at my home. It was not my plan to open a school and then urge them to come to it and learn. Rather I planned to grow slowly into their lives so that they would come to me and ask for the school.[3]

This is a long and beautiful story. This is not the place to set down just how, and over what obstacles, Miss Najafi managed to bring to Sarbandan the clinic, the girls' school, the use of sterilized water, the new bath. Our concern now is to answer: how did she go about winning the confidence of the community? Let us not expect to identify a specific *technique* which we can learn—one, two, three—and apply when we face similar circumstances. We might as well try to put down in cold type the "technique" for making love. How does one win the confidence of another? It is first of all an act of *being*, not doing.

We *can* say that Mr. Leet's way of going about it was different from Miss Najafi's. You would have to know Leet to understand. I worked with him for three years at the United Nations. Why is it that some people have the knack (and others do not) of simply quietly *being* with the result that others find themselves impelled to pour out their enthusiasms or their needs. Can the knack be acquired? Probably, but we might as well try to put in print how to paint a picture. Of course the face expresses sincere interest, and there must be mutual respect. *You* spell out the rest if you can. That's as far as I can go. However, there is one thing Glen Leet *did* that we can itemize. In addition to remaining passive and being a good listener, showing a sincere interest, he demonstrated his trust in the villagers by the gesture of leaving a token deposit of money in their care to start the work.

As we study Miss Najafi's way of approaching her village, we may be tempted to conclude that she had an advantage over Leet in that she was also a Persian. This had little to do with her success. Here is a girl of wealthy urban parents. She leaves her city home in Teheran to be educated in America at Pasadena City College in California. The social and cultural gulf between her and the average villager in Sarbandan was as wide as between Glen Leet and the first Korean farmer that he met. In most of the newly developing countries this wide gulf exists between the small elite at the top and the multitude at the bottom. Bridging this gulf between those who might lead and those who need leadership is the main task with which we are here concerned. Carl C. Taylor has written:

Taylor on "The Agent of Change"

There has been a lot of study and analytical description of how the villager refuses to change and explanations of why he will not change, but there has been very little research on why and how he changes when he does. From what little recorded data there are on these issues, and from observations of and interviews with a great many villagers who have changed and who are changing, I believe some valid conclusions can be drawn. I believe it can be said that most villagers will and do change to new practices if and when they are sure that these practices will give them more production with the same or less effort. They will change if they are convinced that some new practice will keep them and members of their family from dying or from becoming ill. They will change if they believe they can improve their status with their neighbors. They live day by day, however, very near the margin or point of mere survival, and to change is always dangerous. They are not sufficiently sophisticated, or maybe we should say so gullible, as to accept advice about change from a stranger. The job of inducing or stimulating them to change must be done by someone whom they know and trust, and even then, the change must be in activities with which the villager, almost by necessity, is vitally concerned. The agent of change, whoever he may be, needs to know and appreciate these facts and had better be sure that the changes he suggests will produce quite readily obvious and early results.

The job to be done at the other end of this line of cultural traffic between the villagers and the personnel of technical departments of government is the development of an adequate corps of trained scientists and technicians in the fields in which the major problems of villagers exist. In most underdeveloped countries, there is no such adequately trained corps of personnel. Much of the science they know is quite academic, and few of the scientists have technical skills to match their scientific knowledge. Most of them do not know, and do not know they need to know, villagers. Many of them have never worked with their hands, even in the laboratory, much less in the field. I am inclined to believe that the task of inducing or stimulating them to change their behavior and attitudes is as great as, or greater than, it

I believe I have observed in countries quires some meeting between these two ffic that it is harder to come down from om the bottom.

ntries, the two-way line of communica-ned technicians has to be developed *de novo.* In no underdeveloped country is it adequate or functioning on a day-by-day basis. Such lines as exist, and such substations as are on these lines, were established for the administrative functions of collecting taxes and maintaining law and order. The personnel who man these lines and way-stations are neither enough in number nor adequately trained. The consequences are that an understanding of villagers and village problems does not effectively travel from the bottom to the top, and technical know-how does not effectively travel from top to bottom. If there is to be effective two-way communication over this administrative line, some of the substations on the line must be located nearer to villages and some must be near the central sources of technical know-how.[4]

Miss Najafi was such a "substation." She had the advantage of going to live in the village. She was of the same religion as the villagers, but let us not exaggerate this advantage. The conventional practice of religious ritual does not necessarily unite people or establish confidence between them, though they worship in the same mosque, church, or temple. What *does* unite is a common yearning to come closer to the Great Mystery. It is this common yearning and common need which unites men even across barriers of different ritual and dogma. I think that the villagers felt Miss Najafi's complete sincerity and her spiritual approach to understanding their problems and that this established confidence, although her conception of the Deity may actually have been far different from theirs.

One tiny bit of her "technique" we can identify. When she came to the village she was not dressed in the gay raiment of her fellow picnickers. She "was dressed in the black silk duster, the long black gloves, the head scarf of the traveler." When I visited a Quaker volunteer work camp in Ocampo, Mexico, I found all the young men of the Friends' unit wearing the same footgear as the men of the village beside whom they were doing pick-and-shovel work. This was a homemade sandal, the sole carved out of an automobile tire. I was told that the wearing of shoes marks as a city aristocrat. The girls of the Friends' unit all wore skirts, although at home in the United States they would probably have worn blue-jean trousers to work in. So careful were they not to offend the mores of the village that even when on a holiday they all climbed Mt. Popocatepetl, they still wore their less convenient skirts. I was told of another international organization which was operating volunteer work camps which encouraged the girls to wear whatever they would have worn at home with the idea of "educating" the village girls to adopt a freer mode of dress. I am inclined to believe that had the young Friends of the girls' unit at Ocampo been so arrayed, they would not have been accepted in the homes where they were acting as nurses' aides.

However, this matter of dress cannot be a hard-and-fast rule. For example: when, later during her stay in Sarbandan, Miss Najafi planned to visit the various homes:

I dressed carefully for my visits. I did not wear the dress of the women of Sarbandan; that would have been effrontery. The dress belonged to them and I was a stranger. I put on a full long skirt of bright print, a long-sleeved, high-necked blouse that matched it. Over my hair I put a kerchief.

I suspect that one must have a feeling for matters of this kind and cannot follow a fixed rule. The only guide is probably a sincere sensitivity to the feelings of others.

How to find out significant facts about the community without house-to-house inquiries

Karimpur, India

We sat on the running board of our motor and contemplated the village across the road. We had chosen Karimpur as being reasonably typical of the villages in our section of the United Provinces. We had secured credentials from higher quarters and had been officially introduced to the Patwari, the village accountant in the employ of the Government. We had found an old mango grove; and therein had set up tents for our helpers, ourselves, and our two small sons. And now we were ready to study the village. But would the village permit itself to be studied?

. . . . .

We came . . . to make a survey of the social, religious, and economic life of a fairly typical North India village; we were bent upon gathering facts by the most direct methods possible. But our new neighbors were not prepared for anything so rapid or impersonal.

. . . . .

Our clerk brought in the news that after observing our camp, and considering the various rumors that arrived in advance, the leaders of the village had concluded that the Sahib (Mr. Wiser) must be . . . someone interested in taxes. Our clerk had tried to assure them that we were here on a helpful mission. . . . They were running no risks with unlabeled strangers. . . . And yet, our work depended on the co-operation of these, our new neighbors. We had to win their confidence and friendship or roll up our tents and move on.

Early the next morning, a tall figure carrying a closely wrapped bundle appeared from the corner of the village where outcasts lived and ventured across the muddy road. He was a Christian. He had heard somewhere that we were missionaries, and he knew from experience that missionary visitors in tents were not to be feared. He brought his baby, suffering from dysentery, for treatment. We had a medical kit for family emergencies and from this we gave him medicine for the baby, along with a bit of homemade advice on feeding. As he recrossed the road, neighbors peered from several doorways waiting to see him or his child collapse (as they have laughingly confessed to us since).

. . . . .

From the Patwari, we secured the names of the four men who could help us most if they chose. The Sahib called on these, was greeted with hospitable offers of milk, fuel, and even beds. But to intimations of a Social Survey, there was a guarded response. We had not before realized how difficult it would be to explain the purpose of a Study to a practical villager. . . .

Our introduction from District officials could secure for us every physical comfort, but not the co-operation we desired. Experience has taught the villager to conceal his wealth and to avoid any revelation of his true status, lest it be used later to his disadvantage. A direct question at once arouses his suspicion. And without his confidence we could only hope for distortions of the truth.

We set ourselves the task of turning opposition into confidence, and fear into friendship. We had not known it, but the Christian father with his child was our first step. His baby did not die as anticipated by neighbors but improved. On the following morning we found three daring fathers with ailing children at our tent door. On the following day there were ten, then twenty, then fifty. Half of the office tent was transformed into a dispensary.

The previous summer in the hills, the Memsahiba (Mrs. Wiser) had heard a lecture on medical helps for those working in villages. The notes from this lecture were brought out and used until the pages were in tatters. Our medical supplies were rapidly exhausted and had to be replenished by frequent trips to town. We acquired another tent to be used as a dispensary and established one clerk in it with instructions for simple treatments, while we occasionally withdrew to the office tent for study. At times, the Survey threatened to be swamped by prolonged hours of amateur medical service. But these hours served our purpose, as few activities could have done. Fathers, and the few mothers who dared come, became communicative, voluble. Opportunities for questioning rapidly increased although weariness, and pity for unnecessary suffering, often blotted out our desire to seek information. First Aid and Home Nursing had not appeared in our Survey schedule, or budget. But they proved our greatest asset—and expense. And they will remain necessary items in any effort at village service, until village folk learn to protect themselves from the preventable diseases which now travel freely from town to town and house to house.[5]

Does this experience of Mr. and Mrs. Wiser help us to answer the question: "How do we find out significant facts about the community without house-to-house inquiries?" I think it does. House-to-house inquiries would have obviously been impossible until they had (a) won the confidence of the community and (b) authenticated themselves as belonging in the community by rendering some service regarded as important by the villagers. Nor do I

think there was any other way to find out such significant facts
until they had met these two prerequisites. But the record shows
that the moment they rendered first aid medical service, the significant facts for their Survey were available to them with a minimum
of direct inquiry. In more sophisticated communities it may be
possible for a community worker to begin his work by conducting
a direct Survey as formally organized and conducted as the United
States Census. I doubt if that would ever be possible in more
primitive communities. The worker must be content to begin to
serve without gathering all the facts he wishes in advance. Thereafter his research can be conducted steadily although mainly by
indirection.

This conclusion is borne out by the experience of Miss Najafi in
Sarbandan which was very similar to the experience of the Wisers.

Sarbandan (continued)

I knew that I had much to learn and that I would have to learn as I
worked, but I was determined to start out in an orderly way. Although
I did not know well the strange sea I had embarked on, nevertheless I
needed to chart my course and decide upon my destination. Carefully I
drew a map of the village. On it I placed every home. Starting from the
west and moving toward the east, street by street, alley by alley, house
by house, I would visit every home. Sometime, and that very soon, I
would know the names of everyone in the village. I would know which
families were rich, which ones were poor, which ones owned land,
which were tenant farmers, actually almost serfs left over from an
outmoded feudal system. Each night after a day of visits I could check
off the houses I had visited on the master map and add to my case-
history files information about each family. It would have been easier,
I know, to start in haphazard fashion, visiting those who lived near me,
but that way I would have immediately aroused the feeling that some
were favored, others were not. Now if people asked me why I had not
visited their home I could explain that I wasn't yet on their street, that
when the turn came I would be there.

The map looked beautiful on paper, the plan that I would follow seemed businesslike and perfect. I had forgotten how strong ignorance, suspicion, fear could be. Or perhaps I thought that because I was a Moslem and loved the people suspicion would not wall me out.

. . . . .

You do not knock on the door in Sarbandan. There are no doors. "Yoo-hooh. Anybody in?" I called at the first house.

"Who is there?" came the question in an almost sullen voice.

"I am Lady Najafi," I answered. "I am a teacher."

"I am Eshrat. Come in, my lady," the voice answered.

I went in, my eyes growing accustomed to the darkness. The walls, the floor were of dried earth. The woman who peered at me through slitted, suspicious eyes was feeding a young child from a bowl about which the flies buzzed in a humming spiral.

Sanitation, I thought. *God, put words in my mouth.*

She brushed at the flies with a careless hand. "Flies," she said. "Always flies in the summertime."

"Yes," I said, thoughtfully. "But there is a way to kill the flies." I thought of the latrines of Sarbandan, too few, too seldom used; of human excrement being used to fertilize the fields, of animal filth in every dooryard. "There is a spray," I told her. "Material called DDT. I have used it at my home and it is very good."

Her eyes passed from my kerchief to my simple sandals and came to rest on her own rough bare feet. "If I had what you have I'd kill flies, too," she said with growing sullenness.

"You may use my spray," I offered.

. . . . .

Finally, when I left, the woman had consented to borrow my spray. In my plan for the day I had allowed fifteen minutes for each call. With my first woman I had spent an entire morning. I went back to my home, got out my map of the village and checked the house. On my case history I wrote, "Suspicious, somewhat crafty. She is a complex character. She both loves and hates, both hungers for knowledge and fears it."

I did not know how many times I was going to write those words after a name.

It was midafternoon when I stopped at the home of Fatemeh. There was no answer to my call, no sign of life when I peered inside the house. Somewhere I could hear the mewing of a sick child. I went around to the back. A slender young woman, dressed in a bright cotton print, holding a whimpering child in her arms, was bent over a black kettle hanging above an open fire.

"Salaam," I said quietly. She didn't turn, just kept on stirring. "May I help you?"

She turned her face toward me. There was a look of complete despair in her red-rimmed eyes and I could trace the tracks of tears down her smoke-grayed face. I took the child from her arms and looked down into his yellowing face. He was six months old perhaps, but unbelievably thin and dry-skinned.

"He isn't going to die. Six I have had that died, but Ali will live!" There was hysteria in her voice. "I won't let him die!"

"What are you making?" I watched her rough hand, white-knuckled around the shapeless iron spoon.

Her glance at me said, "Why, you stupid woman! How is it that you don't know?" Her lips said defiantly, "Medicine."

"And what is this medicine?"

"The blood of a living raven boiled with crushed beetles." Her eyes, wide with fear, came to my face for a minute. "It is a good medicine?"

"No, no no!" I wanted to cry out. "It is not a good medicine!" Instead I said as calmly as I could, "It is a strange medicine for one so small. So helpless."

I did not know how to answer her. All I knew was that I must save this little one from that horrible brew. I moved to overturn the kettle, but I stopped myself. What right had I to do this? The baby's father had probably spent hours in snaring a living raven so that the blood could drip from it while it still lived.

I reached for the child and the mother put him in my arms. Think of something, think of something, I told myself as I hushed him against my breast.

· · · · ·

In the tiny village of Japon, about five or six kilometers from Sarbandan, the government had opened a small, well-stocked clinic. I did not know who was in charge there. I didn't even know that I knew there was a clinic, but I trusted this moment of inspiration. "Come," I said. "You hold the baby and I will go rent a donkey. We will take him to a doctor." . . . I described the cough. "Croup," he said, "with a respiratory infection." He studied the yellow face, the yellow eyeballs of the child. "Give plenty of boiled water and as much milk as he will take," he said. The mother put her hands on her shrunken breasts, a mute gesture that said the milk had left her breasts and she could not feed the child.

The doctor put a package of dried milk into my hands. "You'll know what to do with this," he said. Then he gave the mother a small bottle of medicine. "When the child coughs give him a dose of this every few minutes until he vomits," he said.

"Vomits?" she questioned.

"Yes, that will clear his throat for breathing." I stole a glance at the medicine. It was ipecac. . . .

When I returned my home was full of women with children in their arms. "You helped Fatemeh's child," they told me. "My child, too, needs help."

So now God had answered my question. I had asked Him where I should begin. Was it to be with education, with industry, with sanitation? Now I knew. Unprepared as I was in the field of medicine I must begin with a clinic.

. . . . .

I thought of the Imperial Organization of Social Services and decided to turn to them for help. . . .

They listened to my problem and approved the formation of a clinic in Sarbandan.

A visitor would have smiled if he hadn't become apprehensive at my lack of knowledge. I learned to give shots: vitamin, antibiotic, penicillin. I got a large medical book with symptoms plainly described. I took the first-aid materials and the simple medicines that were given me. And scared to death, I opened the clinic.

I had been in my little home less than two months and now it was no longer mine. While I was gone on my visits, getting acquainted with the people of my village, the sick gathered in my one room. When I returned I had to step over them to reach my medical book, my aspirin tablets, my first-aid supplies that were neatly shelved in one of the alcoves.

"I am not a doctor," I told all of the patients. "I can give only first aid." But they were happy with first aid, especially if a shot was included.[6]

Later, doctor friends of Miss Najafi from Teheran agreed to come to Sarbandan on Fridays to hold an established clinic. The doctors rotated their services so that no one of them had too heavy a burden. Thus, Miss Najafi's efforts to gather and record "significant facts about the community" were interrupted by the villagers' need for health service. Yet indirectly as they came to her for this service she learned these facts.

Nor is it only in primitive villages in the Far East that Social Research must proceed by indirection rather than by formal inquiry. William Foote Whyte was studying, under a Junior Fellowship from Harvard, a slum area which he called "Cornerville" in a large eastern city in the United States. He became acquainted with one of the "corner boys" called "Doc," who then guided him and introduced him around as his friend. Whyte thus describes his experience:

Cornerville, U.S.A.

In my interviewing methods I had been instructed not to argue with people or pass moral judgments upon them. This fell in with my own inclinations. I was glad to accept the people and to be accepted by them. However, this attitude did not come out so much in interviewing, for I did little formal interviewing. I sought to show this interested acceptance of the people and the community in my everyday participation.

I learned to take part in the street corner discussions. . . .

Sometimes I wondered whether just hanging on the street corner was an active enough process to be dignified by the term "research." Perhaps I should be asking these men questions. However, one has to learn when to question and when not to question as well as what questions to ask.

I learned this lesson one night in the early months when I was with Doc in Chichi's gambling joint. . . .

The next day Doc explained the lesson of the previous evening. "Go easy on that 'who,' 'what,' 'why,' 'when,' 'where' stuff, Bill. You ask those questions, and people will clam up on you. If people accept you, you can just hang around, and you'll learn the answers in the long run without even having to ask the questions."

I found that this was true. As I sat and listened, I learned the answers to questions that I would not even have had the sense to ask if I had been getting my information solely on an interviewing basis. I did not abandon questioning altogether, of course. I simply learned to judge the sensitiveness of the question and my relationship to the people so that I only asked a question in a sensitive area when I was sure that my relationship to the people involved was very solid.

When I had established my position on the street corner, the data simply came to me without very active efforts on my part. It was only now and then, when I was concerned with a particular problem and felt I needed more information from a certain individual, that I would seek an opportunity to get the man alone and carry on a more formal interview.[7]

How to recognize local leaders and the bases of their leadership

Karimpur (*continued*)

The leaders of Karimpur are so sure of their power that they make no effort to display it. The casual visitor finds little to distinguish them from other farmers. They dress as simply and cheaply as their neighbors, and do no more shouting or scolding. They work as faithfully as any in their fields. The walls enclosing their family courtyards may be high, but are no better kept than those adjoining them, and their entrances are often less elaborate. Yet when one of them appears among men of serving caste, the latter express respect and fear in every guarded word and gesture. The serving ones have learned that as long as their subservience is unquestioned, the hand which directs them rests lightly. But let there be any move toward independence or even indifference among them, and the paternal touch becomes a strangle-hold.

Rights and privileges which would be in the hands of the landlord, were he to reside in the village, are retained by the small group of leaders. The ordinary villager looks to them for advances for his animals and implements. He waters his fields from their wells. The waterways to his fields must pass through their land. His animals graze on areas under their control. He borrows their bullocks in times of need. He has the privilege of collecting fuel from their land. Wood for house and implement repairs, and even the wood for cremating his dead, must be begged from one of them. Money for weddings is borrowed from them. Employment in slack times for some, and full-time employment for others, is supplied by them. Women of the serving classes find part-time work in their homes. Carpenters, potters, cotton carders, and other servers of all castes, are their low-caste dependents, since it is through the village leaders that they obtain work. On each festival day, representatives from dependent families visit the homes of leaders who patronize them, and receive cakes and sweets from the women folk. Thus, in every detail of life have the leaders bound the village to themselves. Their favor may bring about a man's prosperity, and their disfavor may cause him to fail, or may make life so unbearable for him that he will leave the village.

The economic power of the leaders is strengthened by their religious and social influence, as Brahmans. The right of Brahmans to dictate may be challenged in the cities, but their control is absolute in villages. Their birth as Brahmans is evidence of their superiority. Many an important decision in a humble section of the village waits on their sanction. Although they occupy themselves as farmers and grain lenders, two or three of them are called upon to officiate as priests in ceremonies of importance to villagers. As with their economic power they find it unnecessary to proclaim their authority as Brahmans. If anyone fails to recognize the existence of this authority, he is reminded of it so effectively that he does not err again.

He who would help any one group or all groups of the village cannot afford to ignore the power of present leaders. If he sees little hope of securing justice or improved conditions through them, and has sufficient financial support, he can replace them. But he must make the substitution complete. By securing for himself the position of economic master, as he would in case he became the landlord or financial agent, he can transfer all rights and duties of leadership to himself.

A missionary in Moradabad has done this with marked success. He has freed his people from the all-encompassing indebtedness to the old leaders by transferring their dependence at every point to a co-operative society under his direct guidance. They still acknowledge a leader. They have been led so long that they would flounder if suddenly obliged to act on their own responsibility and make important decisions unguided. But their new leader is concerned with their welfare and the development of their independence, rather than their subordination. Though nominally a co-operative society, this method makes heavy demands upon the time and finances of the leader. It also involves the personal supervision of a number of highly qualified co-leaders. But it is the fairest and surest form of replacement.

Partial replacement is more doubtful, and may prove harmful to those whom it aims to help. Like leaders everywhere, village leaders are jealous of their power. If they find someone attempting to usurp their rights, without paying the price, their suspicions are naturally aroused. If they discover that a villager is being drawn away from them at any one point, they become antagonistic toward the agency which is drawing him, and eventually devise some means of forcing him back. This accounts for the failure of many a co-operative credit society which has reached past the leaders and drawn its membership from dissatisfied followers. A villager accepts financial help from such a society. He pays his old debts to his leader, and promises to incur no new debts, except to the society. But he must still turn to his old leader for many favors, such as grazing ground for his animals, water for his fields, and perhaps employment for his sons. Some urgent need for money may then arise, which he finds is beyond the scope of the society. He turns to the old leader, whose rules for loans are more flexible. He thinks that he can pay up and still carry on as a member of the society. But the leader's grip has tightened and will not let him go. He is drawn back into the old order, and the service of the co-operative society is futile.

Where co-operative societies have been introduced with the support of established leaders, their chances of success have been greater. Leaders who are approachable and who have had a chance to discover what co-operation can accomplish, have not only helped, but in some cases have themselves developed the work of the societies. The rural reconstruction and the better-living societies of the Benares district, which include a whole village in a group, have served well, with the support of existing leaders. These societies have not limited themselves to credit nor any one phase of agriculture, but have fostered the development of the community as a whole, helping and strengthening it, through adult education, better marketing, improved sanitation, or any other service which may be performed co-operatively.

This or a similar method of co-operation, which includes rather than replaces existing leaders, is more desirable if the leaders are willing to co-operate. By sharing with them what we have learned of community welfare, we can help them to a more altruistic application of their power. They cannot be expected to change from selfish motives to community interests immediately. But once they care for the well-being, rather than the subservience of their dependents, they can do more than outsiders can hope to do.

. . . . .

The average farmer listens with interest to an explanation of the advantages of a new variety of seed. But he would not risk trying it unless his leader first tried it, or at least sanctioned it. He might be an enthusiastic observer of the demonstration of a Persian wheel used for drawing water, but he could not afford to buy one without a loan from his leader; and he would not think of asking for a loan until his leader had himself installed a wheel. He knows that if he should presume to supersede his leader in any detail, social or economic, he would be brought down forcibly to his proper station. It is his lot to wait for the signal to advance. He has learned from experience that the cool judgment of his leader can save him from the mistakes into which his own gullibility is apt to plunge him. These simple village folk can be helped most if the confidence and approval of their leaders is won, even though in so doing advantages are granted to the leaders which seem beyond their deserts.

The official revival of the authority of the village *Panchayat* is an acknowledgment of the power of the leaders. *Panchayats* have been adopted in several areas after other experiments in village service have been tried out. The *Panchayat* involves the maximum co-operation of the leaders. While acting on the *Panchayat* as representatives of the village, they are expected to consider the order and well-being of the community, rather than personal ambitions.

The burden of village responsibility rests on the leaders, just as family responsibility rests on the head of the house. The moment a villager finds himself harassed by a landlord seeking payment of rent arrears, or by the police implicating him in a dacoity case, he comes to his leader, as a son to his father, expecting the necessary help, financial or otherwise. Like a father, the leader intercedes and makes whatever settlement is demanded, on behalf of his dependent. It may demand days away from pressing field work, interviewing officials, and attending court. It may involve the expenditure of a considerable number of rupees. But the leader gives and does all ungrudgingly, as part of his responsibility.[8]

Let us now contrast this example with a quite different one from Mexico:

Ocampo, Mexico

In the autumn of 1953, the American Friends Service Committee established a service unit or work camp in a small village east of Mexico City. The group consisted of eight young men and four young women. They were housed in the only two-story house in the village. The house belonged to the Senator from that district. He had been born in that village. He belonged to the "PRI" (the "Party of the Revolution") which was in control of the Mexican government. The Senator had become rich and powerful and lived in Mexico City. He had built a rather pretentious two-story house in the village for his old mother, but she preferred to remain in her adobe house and live like the rest of the villagers. As the new house was vacant, it was offered to the Friends.

The Senator and the Governor of the state (both of whom belonged to the PRI) had invited the Friends to establish a work camp in the village. The girls of the group were to work with the state health authorities assisting the nurses and doctors in administering injections and vaccinations and spraying with DDT.

For the young men of the work camp, the main project was co-operation with the villagers in rebuilding the road through the village. It was hoped that the state would then build a bridge over the river, connecting the hamlet with the main road to the state capital. When the Friends Service Unit arrived in the village, the road resembled a miniature Grand Canyon, impassable for motor transport. If the condition of this village street were improved, a bus service might be started, and the sick would no longer have to be carried on a litter, or have to walk to receive medical attention.

Until the bridge was built, however, it would still be necessary, in driving from the nearby city (which lay just across the river to the south of the village) to go four miles east, then five miles north where the highway crossed the river on a modern bridge, and then double back along the river to the point where the road through the village became impassable.

The local chairman of the PRI drew up a list of men available for work on the road, one from each household per day. This provided ten men, plus eight from the Friends service unit, a sizable force for the pick and shovel work of restoring the road. Soon a number of men from the village dropped out until finally only the Friends unit was left. This demoralized the latter, who came to co-operate with the villagers, rather than toil alone. They talked to the local chairman of the PRI, who promised that twenty men would appear the following day. On the contrary the villagers said they were busy with their crops and could not spare the time to work on the road at that time of the year.

As the members of the service unit became more and more accepted into the community, news as to the real reason for lack of co-operation on the road project percolated through to them. There were four political parties in the village, all opposed to the PRI. One of the political promises of the ruling party in the last election was that, if returned to power, the road would be rebuilt. The other parties did not relish making good their opponent's political promises. To the other villagers, the Friends service unit appeared to be linked to the party in power. They lived in the Senator's house and seemed to be associated with the party officials.[9]

Later, as we shall see in our next chapter, the Friends found a way to overcome this difficulty. We are concerned here with the basis of the Senator's leadership. As his political importance increased nationally and at the state capital, it waned in his native village. Perhaps they were cynical as to the sources of his increasing wealth. The village and the adobe house where he was born were not good enough for him. They probably resented even the fine house he had built in the village which stood empty until the Friends came. Could the Friends have learned that he was no longer a leader to his fellow villagers? Probably not until they had lived for a while among the village people.

Here is another example of a successful man who became no longer a leader:

The Rajasthan Farmer, India

An agricultural expert, working to improve conditions in the state of Rajasthan in India, under a grant from the U.S. International Cooperation Administration, sought to make use of the most successful farmer in the region. He brought other farmers to inspect his successful farm. To his surprise they were not impressed. Apparently they were jealous of this farmer's excellence. Perhaps in the East the drive to excel is not admired as much as in the West. We all know the bright boy in school who does not exert himself lest he become unpopular with his fellows. Evidently leadership has many bases and neither wealth nor ability may prevail if a man is too far ahead of his fellows, so that he has lost touch with them or incurred their jealousy.[10]

*   *   *

Summary. There is no simple technique for winning the confidence of a community. Sincerity is essential, and affection and willingness to listen. Living in the community is desirable. Significant facts are not to be learned by formal inquiry. The inquirer must first be accepted as serving the community. Then the information will follow. On close observation, local leaders are generally recognizable, but the bases of their leadership are various and may not depend on wealth or ability.

III. FELT NEEDS

How can we discover what are the felt needs of the community?

In Ocampo (see Chapter II) it was the Senator and his political associates who advised the Friends to undertake to repair the village street. The people of the village were not consulted. As this was one of the planks in their political opponents' platform, they refused to co-operate. The sequel was as follows:

Ocampo, Mexico (continued)

The Friends unit discussed this difficulty for a long time and finally hit upon a solution: a general meeting of all the villagers was called, where the service unit could explain their aims to the community. The meeting was held at the school, and slides were shown of a member of the village working in his field or making *pulque* from the maguey plant. To most of the Mexicans present, such a slide show was a new experience. The meeting was well attended.

After the slide show, one of the volunteers stated the philosophy of the Friends service unit and their desire to collaborate in whatever projects the villagers thought most important. Most of the villagers wanted to build a bridge across the river, but this could not be done without a substantial appropriation from the Mexican Federal Government. Others suggested digging an irrigation canal to bring water from the river to their parched fields. Still others suggested building additional rooms onto the overcrowded school building, which housed 300 pupils in two rooms.

It was finally agreed to split up the working force into two gangs. One villager, as foreman, led a group of the villagers and some of the Friends to continue work on the road, while another group of villagers and volunteers started the irrigation canal. This was dug so that water from higher up the stream was led inland to water the fields. It was a pick and shovel job which would probably have to be renewed or repaired each year. The canal also brought the washing place (an important center and gossip exchange), formerly by the river, nearer the village. The irrigation canal was completed early in 1954, and plans were made to start on the extra rooms for the school.[1]

Obviously such a meeting of the villagers should have preceded any decision as to what work should be undertaken first. A frequent mistake of those who wish to do something *for*, instead of *with*, a community is to decide what may appear to be most needed without consulting the villagers as to whether they either need it or want it. To be sure, citizens are not always wise as to what is most needed for their good; but, after all, it is *their* community. An outside expert may help by his advice, but the decision must be *theirs*, or little of permanent benefit may result. For example:

Northern Territories, Gold Coast

In the Northern Territories of the Gold Coast a local barber explained to the late Jess Ogden of the University of Virginia the difference between the procedure followed by the British District Officers before World War II and the methods used now by the new Community Development workers. In the old days, the District Officer came to the village and said, "Build sanitary latrines or I'll come back and fine you ten shillings." He then went on his way to the next village. The latrines were built to avoid the fine but never used.

"Now," this barber explained, "these new Community Development workers tell us we must build latrines but they explain why; they show us how; and *work with us* pouring cement and digging holes."[2]

Another group of Friends had an experience in Kenya which was very similar to that in Ocampo, Mexico:

Machakos District, Kenya

The camp was located in the very dry Machakos District fifty miles east of Nairobi, and the project was working with villagers in building much-needed dams to hold back what water came during the brief rainy season.

The second day of work at one dam we had no villagers working with us because they had all believed the rumor that these strangers were being paid by the government. The head man called a big "baraza" or town meeting and finally convinced them that we were really volunteers. From that time on the villagers turned out in dozens, both men and women. The most exciting reward for our rock-breaking, cement-mixing labors was a welcome to an authentic all-night African dance inside a thatch-roofed hut deep in the bush.

Again and again in Africa the interest in international voluntary work camping and the eagerness to participate . . . in projects far exceeded the opportunities available. The need to expand these opportunities is urgent for many reasons. Such projects can spark increased village self-help efforts. They can promote the dignity of manual labor and respect for women. They can save the students from intellectual snobbishness, for they increase sympathetic understanding and solidarity with the still uneducated rural majority, who need their leadership and concern. By helping to overcome tribal, linguistic, and religious barriers such projects promote national unity—perhaps above all, they can promote much-needed interracial good will, if only white people can be persuaded to join—and some can.[3]

Someone concerned with Community Development has complained of "the difficulty of getting villagers to feel a felt need!"

We shall consider in the next chapter when and how it is wise and possible to stimulate an *appreciation of need*. Let us record here our conviction that until a substantial, influential number of the community feel the need enthusiastically, the enterprise should not be started. The movement must be *theirs* and not merely the plan (however wise) of some outside expert.

How can a community decide priorities in meeting felt needs?

New Amirpur, India

In 1942 the people of New Amirpur were driven from their original village by a flood of the Damodar River, so the entire village went to settle in what is now their home. They were faced with many difficult problems as they had to start life all over again and build a new village from nothing. In their old village, there had been a traditional panchayat. Its principal functions had been to organize *jatras* and *pujas* on religious occasions, but it had also done some community work such as cleaning tanks and clearing roads.

When they moved to New Amirpur, some of the people felt that they should have a temple. Finally one of their leaders called some meetings of the village to discuss this idea. After discussion, the people decided to get together and build a temple. Before they were finished they built not one but three temples—one large one and two small ones. When we asked the villagers why they had decided to start by building a temple, one of them replied, "How could we move here and leave our Gods behind?"

The next group project which they undertook was the sinking of a tubewell for the village. But all the time they had been thinking that what they really needed was a road from their village to the Grand Trunk Road. Six years ago they had approached the Sub-Divisional Officer and the administrative department for help in building this road; however, they had had little success. Then in 1951 they went to the Agriculture Department in their area to ask for help. They said, "We are all farmers, we produce milk and milk products and we need a road in order to market them." Some officers from the Agriculture

Department visited the village and tried to get them to take some action on their own initiative, but the lack of funds seemed too much of an obstacle. Nevertheless, one officer who visited them at that time felt that they had very strong determination.

In February, 1955 the road was finally started with the help of the Community Development Department and it was completed before the rainy season. They were able to secure Rs.250/ —from the Community Development Project—and with this they hired some labor, and the rest of the work was done by them on a voluntary basis. The road is a good dirt (Kutcha) road, one mile long which goes through what was formerly jungle.

When we asked the villagers what benefits they had received since building the road, they immediately listed several items: (1) Formerly there was a footpath through the jungle and they had often suffered from torn clothes and snake-bites. Now they can reach the main road in a few minutes. (2) Now they are able to get their milk products to market easily. (3) Building materials are much cheaper because they can be brought to the village by lorry. For example, they are now building a brick schoolhouse. (4) In case of need a doctor can easily be brought from (Burdwan) town. (5) Formerly they were unable to get teachers from outside, but now two teachers come by cycle from Burdwan. (6) Now they have many more visitors and many more social functions in the village.

At present they are engaged in building a sizable brick school. They raised the money for the school in this manner: After the paddy harvest they secured paddy from each family according to its economic condition. Then they borrowed 50 maunds of paddy from a wealthy cultivator in a neighboring village on a "sawai" basis. That is, they promised to repay one maund and ten seers for each maund [a maund is approximately 80 pounds; a seer, about two pounds] borrowed. This they will do after the next paddy season. One of the members of their village signed the note for this loan. These 50 maunds were sold in the market for Rs.500/—and the money is being used for the school. Also some villagers contributed palm trees and lent their carts for transporting materials for the school. They wanted some corrugated iron sheets for the roof and approached the Project Executive Officer, but he told them that it might take as long as three years to get these sheets. Therefore, they bought asbestos sheets at almost double the price, because they were determined to finish the school. They have also bought two water-seal latrines for use in the school. Recently they passed a resolution in their village meeting that each family will have a latrine, but they will not take this up until the school is finished. Their interest in latrines is a result of their having seen some filmstrips on Hookworm which were shown by the Village-Level Worker.

We asked them how they had done these things. They replied that they had frequent group discussions of the whole village in the evenings. At these discussions they decided together what projects they would undertake. The procedure is this: First they have free discussion in which everyone participates. Often there are heated arguments. If some people do not understand why a project is necessary, they are asked to give their reasons. Then these are discussed. When it seems that most people are in agreement, they decide to act.[4]

We must admit that from the standpoint of an outside expert this ranking of priorities of need may not seem logical. Less religious people would not have built three temples before sinking a well or building the road. Again a desire to enhance the prestige or status of the community may outweigh more practical considerations:

Village Post Office in Ghana

A village of one thousand inhabitants in Ghana, after some stimulation by a community development worker, undertook and completed four projects. The order in which they were undertaken was obviously not that suggested by the outside expert. (1) They built a school building which was badly needed. (2) They built a post office building! (Small communities desire this to give them status.) (3) They built a road. (4) They piped in a water supply.[5]

In many cities and other sophisticated communities the answer to our question ("How can a community decide priorities in meeting felt needs?") might be to employ a social scientist or a town planner to make an exhaustive survey and submit recommendations. However, a better method would be what is called a "community self-study." Libraries in the United States contain many volumes of scientific community surveys with findings and recommendations which have produced no results. Shortly before World War II, Pittsburgh employed an expert in social research, to conduct a thorough study of Pittsburgh's health and welfare needs. He was supplied with a large staff of specialists. The resulting recommendations were rejected by the city, and the staff had to seek elsewhere to get the survey published.

This and similar experiences seem to prove that it is highly important to have a responsible committee of representative citizens sponsor the study. Experts may be used as *advisers*, but the findings and recommendations should be made by the committee. Their very act of adopting and signing the report places on them a responsibility to work for the improvements suggested. It is also important in this type of community self-study that all the arts of publicity be employed as the study progresses to keep the community informed and get them to participate. A research scientist works quietly and gives little publicity to his work until it is completed. On the other hand, a community self-study is an experiment in interpretation through participation and should involve as many citizens as possible as it goes along. In Chapter VI we shall study how to organize and operate such a community self-study. It is sufficient to point out here that the "free discussion," with everyone participating in New Amirpur, approximated a community self-study. Such a study may be conducted without outside experts. The resulting decisions may not be so wise as if guided by experts, but they are more likely to result in definite action than a Pittsburgh Survey.

How can community action to meet one felt need result in a chain reaction?

This question has already been partially answered. In the cases cited above from Korea, Iran, Mexico, Ghana, and India completion of the original enterprise sparked community enthusiasm to go on and meet other needs by voluntary effort.

Suh Kam Chon (continued)

Suh Kam Chon is a village where several years ago the farmers had been motivated to restore their irrigation works. It took thousands of man-hours. Following the floods last year, villagers again had to de-silt their clogged canals—but this time they did it without any outside help at all. In addition, idle land has been reclaimed for rice paddy. . . . Labor and income from the rice crop increment had been invested in child welfare—a playground. Jim Mook Lee, the Save-the-Children-Federation community development specialist in Korea, reports that at the playground he now sees "many children playing cheerfully."

All current projects of the Suh Kam Chon pattern were being actively pursued this spring since paddy fields need to be watered starting in May. An exception of sorts was in the large-scale project at Tae Chun Ri. This enrolled co-operation of the government since a large permanent concrete dam was part of the scheme. Jim Mook Lee took the officials concerned to see what the villagers had accomplished in building dikes and canals, and helped in putting through the papers to get the government's promised contribution of cement for the dam. Two hundred bags of cement were delivered early in June.[6]

Here is another illustration of a similar chain reaction in an Indian village:

Chotapara, India

The village (let us call it "Chotapara," since it consists of only 40 households) is located about 60 miles from Calcutta. There is a road which winds through the center of the village, and each year, at the time of the monsoon, the villagers used to talk about the need for improving the road. During the rainy season it presented a real problem to the community. After a little rain there was so much mud that it was difficult to walk or drive a bullock cart over it. Besides, dirty water used to collect in the ditches along the road and run off into the village tank polluting the water. Though discussion of this problem was an annual event in "Chotapara," it had never culminated in constructive action until a Gram Sevak (village worker) was posted in the area.

The Gram Sevak began to focus their attention more on this problem and suggested that it was possible for the villagers to do something about it. At first they paid little attention to him. Then, as he became better known, the villagers began to realize that "this fellow was speaking correctly." So meetings were called to discuss what could be done; in one month during the monsoon as many as ten were held. Still the community was not ready to go ahead with the work. After one year and a half during which meetings were held from time to time with gradually more and more people participating, it was decided to take action to improve the road. According to the villagers about "five annas" ($1/3$) of the village were involved at the beginning of the actual road construction project. Gradually more people joined until there was participation by almost 90 per cent of the people of the village.

Earth and ashes were put on the road to fill the ruts and raise the level. Prior to this, the villagers say, they could hardly walk barefoot on this road because of the deep mud, but now they can go with their shoes on. In addition, the improved road makes it possible for their children to attend the school in a nearby village.

After completing the earthwork, the villagers began to bring stone chips by bullock cart in order to give the road a harder surface, but this work has been delayed because in the meanwhile they have decided to build a school. When the school is completed, they intend to finish surfacing the road. In addition to this project, with the help of the Community Development Block staff, a Co-operative Credit Society has also been started for the purpose of giving small loans to the cultivators. One side effect of this community action in "Chotapara" has been that four or five neighboring villages, after having seen the improved road, have decided to improve their own roads.

This is an example of an ordinary village which had obvious felt needs which could be met with the resources of the villagers themselves. However, they needed the help of the Gram Sevak in order to crystallize the need and move from awareness to action in solving their problem. Having dealt successfully with the problem of improving their road, they were encouraged to go on and undertake other community projects such as the school and the Credit Co-operative. This story emphasizes the importance of having one successful experience with a group self-help project. It also illustrates the need for patience in using the Community Development approach. Although all of the villagers may not be involved in the first stage of an action project, after the work begins, more people will join. Finally it illustrates the spreading effect of community action to neighboring villages.[7]

Here is another example of chain reaction—in Kenya this time. It will be noted that the outside experts did not begin with a felt need agreed upon by the villagers and had difficulty at first in getting the inhabitants to accept the results of the social survey. Note also the demonstration conducted by one farmer as a means of convincing the other villagers of the value of the new methods.

Manyassi, Kenya

The district team selected a shallow valley known as Manyassi which ran down to a lake, around the shores of which there had previously been much sleeping sickness. The fly, however, had been removed by the clearing of the bush, and the area resettled. It is, nevertheless, a poor area and the soil is sandy. It was decided to organize a campaign for the general improvement of agriculture and health in the valley. First of all, the District Officer (Community Development) was instructed to carry out a social survey so that it might form the basis for planning the scheme. The survey was carried out successfully, though it aroused a certain amount of suspicion in the early stages. This was allayed by long and patient discussion between the District Officer and the inhabitants.

The survey revealed that many of the able-bodied men were out of the district at work for long periods, since the valley was suited only for a subsistence economy. The methods of animal husbandry and agricultural practices were primitive, the villages were filthy, and the people were mostly illiterate.

The district team studied the report and decided to begin by concentrating on teaching the people to construct cattle bomas or enclosures. The object of this scheme was to change the local practice of pegging out the cattle all over the village enclosure, which had resulted in the manure being scattered widely and put to no useful purpose. [Also] it encouraged the breeding of flies and consequently the spread of disease. The construction of the bomas would make it possible to stack manure mixed with weeds and rubbish cleared from the village enclosure, with the object of eventually spreading it on the land.

The team also decided to work for the planting of live wash-stops to prevent erosion. A local aloe was chosen for this purpose. A subsidiary scheme was to arrange for a system of rotational grazing by closing areas in turn.

Other measures which were proposed were the construction of outside kitchens with improved homemade stoves raised off the ground, to replace the traditional three stones so dangerous to children; the digging of latrines; and improved water supplies.

· · · · ·

The only material assistance proposed was the provision of nails for the construction of the cattle bomas.

· · · · ·

When the people had fully understood the implications (explained by the District Officer) and had promised their support, the scheme was put into operation. A demonstration boma was made in one village by the owner himself, the lines for live wash-stops were pegged out, and a model kitchen was built. The inhabitants came to watch and returned to their villages to practice what they had seen. No village was obliged to carry out the improvements, but many did so. A spirit of rivalry and competition grew up and by the end of the year thirty cattle bomas, some miles of live wash-stops, and many improved kitchens and latrines had been built. . . .

Even more remarkable was the scheme's influence in the surrounding areas. Over one hundred cattle bomas were put up without any material assistance or prompting by the development team. This was brought about simply through the example of the benefits derived in the valley from the innovations, and from a general awakening of initiative.[8]

This chain-reaction phenomenon is the conclusive answer to those who say that such volunteer self-help projects would not be necessary "if the government did what it should for its people." Such paternalism by the central government does not spark a desire in the local community to go on and meet new needs by itself. Rather, it breeds a habit of waiting for further largesse from the government which may not be forthcoming. Furthermore, what the people build themselves is appreciated, used, and well cared for. The latrine built by the government, or by compulsion, may remain unused.

*   *   *

Summary.   The felt needs of a community may best be discovered by free discussion in meetings of all the inhabitants. Priorities may well be decided in the same manner. Outside experts may advise, but decisions made without the co-operation of the citizens are less likely to have permanent results. One successful experience of meeting community needs by volunteer efforts generally results in a chain reaction by which further needs are met by self-help, resulting in a more self-reliant community.

IV. CATALYSTS

How can a community worker serve as a catalyst to initiate community action?

Housewives, I am told, add to fruit juice which will not jell, a few drops of pectin. In chemistry this is known as a catalytic agent, a substance which (though otherwise inactive) merely by its presence enables action to take place. Glen Leet in Suh Kam Chon (Chapter II) was a catalyst. His presence in Korea, although he was relatively inactive, resulted in community action which continued for many years and spread to many communities. For our purposes in studying community action, the word "enabler" is perhaps a better word than "catalyst"—one who by the stimulation of his presence enables others to perform satisfactorily. The best example of such an "enabler" which I ever saw was the following:

Woodhurst Mental Health Society, U.S.A.

When Miss Parker came to Woodhurst as case supervisor of the Family Service Agency she was struck by the fact that there was no agency working for mental health. There were twenty social agencies but no psychiatric social worker and no resident psychiatrist in a city of 150,000.

Someone has said that community action begins when someone says of some civic condition: "Isn't it awful! Come on, let's do something about it." Plenty of us say, "Isn't it awful!" but few of us follow that up with exhortation to joint action. What should Miss Parker do? She had at least three courses open to her. In the first place, she could do nothing except say to herself, "Isn't it awful!" It was not her job to do anything about it. She was, after all, only the case supervisor of a family agency. If Woodhurst liked conditions this way it was *their* town.

In the second place, she could write to the newspapers or could seek an opportunity to speak on the subject before the Business and Professional Women's Club or some church groups. She had been trained as a psychiatric social worker and was in touch with the National Association for Mental Health from which source she could obtain useful facts and figures.

She chose a third course and a procedure which anyone anywhere seeking to initiate community action might well follow. First, she talked the matter over with Mr. Bristow, the executive of her agency. He was not as well trained as Miss Parker, having been chosen more because he was a man than because of his training. (Men social workers were rare at that time.) Mr. Bristow decided that the matter should be discussed with the board of directors of the agency. (Perhaps Miss Parker tactfully hinted that the matter be taken to a board meeting, but Mr. Bristow always thought it was his own idea.)

Now notice this bit of technique which we might all copy when we wish to awaken our community to a new idea demanding concerted action. In the beginning the idea of awakening Woodhurst to some mental health service was held by only one person (Miss Parker) but now it had become also Mr. Bristow's idea. So now there were two sponsors and soon there would be more, and it would no longer be just Miss Parker's idea. This is important! Contained in this tiny bit of technique is the sound beginning of any successful campaign for community action. This is what followed: Mr. Bristow having agreed to take the matter to the board now had to prepare himself to do so. Miss Parker had no intention of being the spokesman at that meeting,

nor did Mr. Bristow wish that, for it would show his ignorance of the
subject. Suddenly he wanted to know all about the mental health
movement although, an hour before, he couldn't have cared less. This
was just what Miss Parker wanted. Immediately she became helpful
and placed at his disposal a great deal of printed material about mental
health, giving him the general impression that they were studying the
matter together, not that *she* was educating *him*.

And now came the board meeting. Mr. Bristow had learned his
lesson well and made a good job of presenting the matter. Once or
twice he called on Miss Parker to supplement what he was saying and
she did this very well but not so well that she took the credit from Mr.
Bristow. The vice-chairman of the board was Mr. Bellwood, a conservative chemical engineer whose wife had had what was called "a
nervous breakdown." He showed keen interest in the subject. Someone,
perhaps inspired by Miss Parker, suggested that the community council
should be asked to make a study to determine whether Woodhurst
needed some mental health service and if so how it should be set up.
The board was unanimous for this idea, and a committee of three was
appointed to interview the executive of the community council. The
chairman of this committee was to be Mr. Bellwood. Why should a
chemical engineer present this matter to the council? Miss Parker
could have done a better job. But of course that would have been
foreign to her purpose of attracting new people into the movement.
There were now at least three people for the cause: Miss Parker, Mr.
Bristow, and Mr. Bellwood. The latter having agreed to present the
matter to the council now really wanted to prepare himself and spent
hours studying the material which had originally been given to Mr.
Bristow by Miss Parker.

Realism compels me to confess that I was the executive of the
council. Of course I should have been aware of this lack of service in
Woodhurst and should have taken steps to do something about it. Miss
Parker never hinted that this was the case. She was present with the
committee when they called at my office but she never said a word
although Mr. Bellwood's presentation of the subject was somewhat
halting and inadequate. However, Mr. Bellwood was also a member of
the executive committee of the council and an influential citizen. The
council brought into being a study committee of nine citizens headed

by Mr. Bellwood. They spent many months enquiring into the need of a mental health society and a mental health clinic for Woodhurst. In this study they were helped by a temporary worker lent them by the state society for mental health. The nine citizens became enthusiastic for the cause and became the nucleus of the Woodhurst Mental Health Society which was formed. They helped to raise money for a clinic and induced the community fund to take over its support.[1]

In the state of Wisconsin where there is frequently heavy snow children like to roll enormous snowballs as large as themselves. Their technique has some similarity to starting community action. First, you must be sure that the snow is warm enough to "pack," otherwise you might as well go back into the house and wait for a warmer day. (If your community is not ready to accept your cause, you will also have to wait.) Next, you make a *small* snowball about as large as a baseball and pack it hard. (This corresponds to the nucleus of three to nine persons that Miss Parker first brought together in Woodhurst.) Then comes the all-important moment! You place your small snowball on the snowfield. If, as it rolls, it attracts more snow to itself you can roll it on, and it will grow in size indefinitely. (In community action, if the central core of interested people has the capacity to attract more citizens into the cause, then the movement has been born! A new civic organism has come into being, with a life within itself capable of growing indefinitely.)

Miss Parker left Woodhurst before the Mental Health Society came into being, but she had done her work and energized enough citizens so that the growth continued. It is still flourishing today. Some who were thus drawn into the movement have gone on to work for mental health in the state and even in the nation. Someone has said that the true test of a good community worker is what continues to happen *after* he has left town.

Here we can push the metaphor of the snowball a little further. Given a downhill slope and a long enough snowfield, the snowball

will roll on enlarging itself indefinitely despite the absence of the
person who gave it the first push. Also when spring comes and the
snow begins to melt, our firm snowball may be found still intact
with bare ground all around it. Similarly in community action the
cohesion and strong enthusiasm of the central group may carry on
through hard times still unimpaired.

Some are inclined to think that this need for a firm central core
of citizen enthusiasm is no longer necessary if the work is to be
carried on by government. Nothing could be further from the
truth. They forget that most of our governmental functions, from
education to fire fighting, began under unofficial auspices much in
the manner observed by de Tocqueville. These functions continue
under government operation only because the original enthusiasm
of a few citizens has been transmitted to the majority of the voters.

In the city of Monroe a farsighted dentist once conceived the
idea that the teeth of school children should be cleaned and cared
for without charge by trained "dental hygienists" employed by the
city. He began to train young women as such "dental hygienists"
and then went directly to the source of governmental power.
Instead of starting slowly and attracting other citizens into the
movement (as did Miss Parker) he went to the "city boss" (the
chairman of the dominant political party). The legend is that in
an hour and a half of eloquent appeal he sold this gentleman on
the idea and even obtained his promise not to play politics with it.
For a brief period Monroe became an example to the world in the
field of dental hygiene. The scheme was copied in other cities as
far west as Portland, Oregon, and even in Rotterdam, Holland.
But meantime it perished in Monroe. The city boss who sponsored
it was deposed following a scandal and died under indictment for
embezzlement of public funds. A depression set in, and an economy administration emasculated the program on grounds of
economy.

Meanwhile another governmental service was facing the same
financial difficulties but it survived. With the aid of the National

Recreation Association, a Monroe Recreation Association was started in a small way under private auspices using much of Miss Parker's technique; and a strong board of directors came into being constituting a central core of enthusiasm, attracting more and more citizens into the movement. After two years of demonstration under a competent staff supported by voluntary contributions, the board obtained an amendment to the city charter constituting themselves the official Monroe Recreation Commission with a municipal appropriation. Then came the depression which wrecked the dental hygiene movement. The new city administration omitted all monies for recreation from the city budget as a "frill." The members of the commission (the cohesive central snowball of the movement) appealed to the voters. They stumped the city, speaking before luncheon clubs and church groups. The newspapers supported the cause, and the city fathers were forced to restore the appropriation. Public recreation, which collapsed in many other cities during those hard times, weathered the depression in Monroe because the movement had been started wisely and had grown gradually and had become strong.

Webster's Unabridged Dictionary gives two definitions of a "community." The first, or geographical community, is "a body of people living in the same place under the same laws." The second definition is " a body of people having common interests." This might be called the psychological community. Of course when we speak of "organizing" a community it is really the latter that we hope to construct. Success consists in organizing a psychological community within the geographical one. If the former becomes strong enough it will carry the latter along with it. This strength depends less upon the initial size of the movement than upon its cohesion and the intensity of the enthusiasm of those sharing this "common interest." Perhaps the greatest example of this process in all history is the inspiring and knitting together of the Twelve Disciples until after their Leader's death his influence continued through them down the ages, organizing the Christian religion and laying a basis for what we call Democracy, a movement so strong that it is still inspiring men of many religions to overthrow entrenched wrong to this day.

Here is an example from Puerto Rico in which the "enabler" or "catalyst" was a social work student:

Yambele, Puerto Rico

Yambele is a small semirural community, a ward of Rio Piedras, the university city of Puerto Rico. It is located on the outskirts of the city, very close to one of the bigger shopping centers and consists of thirteen acres of land divided in small lots and sublet to individual tenants. Its name, Yambele, is actually the Spanish pronunciation given to "Jean Belle," the name of the original French owner of the estate.

In 1954, when the community organization project began, there were 71 families living in Yambele, comprising a total population of 450 persons. The majority of the heads of households were construction workers, and the average income per family was $160 a month. The average educational level of the population was a fourth-grade elementary school preparation.

The great majority of the inhabitants of the community had been living there for a period of five years. They were former residents of urban slums, displaced by a slum clearance program. Instead of living in one of the available public housing projects they preferred to move their houses—literally—from the condemned slum areas to a lot in Yambele because, as they said, these houses were their very own and they could later leave them to their children. Since Yambele did not conform to the zoning and building regulations established by the planning board of Puerto Rico the community was not served with the public utilities of light, water, and sewerage.

Organization of the community started with a request for help by a patient of the Rio Piedras Public Health Unit of the State Department of Health to a social work student of the School of Social Work of the University of Puerto Rico who had been assigned to this agency for his field work. Patient and student had come in contact through a casework relationship concerned with helping the patient in the solution of social problems complicating his illness.

One day in March, 1954, he came to the student's office to express his satisfaction at the help received; at the same time to inquire whether the student could extend his services to the community in general.

The problem as presented by the patient was lack of running water and electricity, as a result of which the neighbors, he said, had to bathe in a contaminated stream and drink impure water out of wells. Many, like himself, had bilharziasis [parasites in the blood]; and the children were suffering from "chronic diarrhea." The patient also told of individual efforts made by several members of the community to find solutions to these problems. One had written the governor asking for help, another had addressed the mayoress of the city government, while a third had presented the situation to the planning board. Since these efforts had been to no avail, the patient was sure that if somebody with influence (which he was sure the student had) interested himself in the problems of the community the solutions could be found.

The student conferred with his supervisor and it was deemed desirable to find out whether the community was conscious of its health needs and whether its members were willing to join their efforts for meeting these needs. Accordingly the student asked the patient if he might call a meeting of the neighbors who had distinguished themselves by their interest in solving the problems.

Ten persons, recognized leaders of the community, attended this first meeting, and they offered to call a mass meeting for the neighbors to discuss their problems in more detail. The student, in turn, planned to bring with him other persons from the health unit who might be of some help.

The student then had individual conferences with the members of the public health team. The medical director approved of the project and stimulated the staff to participate. The field work supervisor attached to the school of social work and a social worker from the staff of the health unit offered to continue helping the community, once the student finished his term at the field work center. The health educator, in turn, offered to participate actively in stimulating the participation of the community in the solution of its public health problems. Both the nurse and the sanitary inspector assigned to the zone were already familiar with the community. The sanitary inspector was engaged in a campaign for the building of latrines, while the nurse had visited the homes of her patients.

When these professionals had been reached through individual interviews, the student called a group conference of the members of the team. Thus an advisory committee was formed. A tentative date was agreed upon for the meeting at Yambele, and it was decided that at this meeting the team would try to find out the scope of the health problems of the community and the possibilities for co-ordinated action.

A mass meeting was held in Yambele on the evening of May 14, 1954, with seventy-five adults present. The number was considered an adequate representation of the community. Some heads of households had excused themselves because they had to work at the time of the meeting.

This served to get a consensus on what the members of the community considered to be their problems, while the consulting staff stressed the importance of pooling their efforts toward solving these problems. In addition to electricity and running water, the neighbors were conscious of the need for adequate recreation facilities, and were worried because so many in the community looked "anemic" (probably suffering from uncinariasis). They also felt that if some classes on child care were given right there in the community, families would improve their health habits, as well as their attitudes toward the children. By the end of the meeting the enthusiasm shown by community members had been conveyed to the consulting staff, and the health educator planned to bring a film showing what another community had done to help itself in the solution of a problem.

The following week the picture *Una Voz en la Montana* (A Voice in the Mountain), produced by the Division of Community Education of the State Department of Education, was shown and the student social worker and the health educator led the discussion of the film. It was felt that the community had grasped the message and that the neighbors were willing to join efforts in solution of their recognized needs.

After another mass meeting in which the preliminary orientation and the definition of health problems was continued, the neighbors elected a "Committee of Leaders for the Welfare of Yambele," which consisted of a president, a secretary, a treasurer, and two representatives of the five most populated sections of the community. Contrary to the student's expectations, his client, who had originally involved him in this project, was not elected president. The community preferred a more influential leader: the storekeeper, who was also the owner of several lots. The patient was chosen as representative of his sector. Another point of interest is that five women were appointed to share the responsibilities of leadership together with eight men.

The committee of leaders met regularly on Tuesday evenings to continue discussion of their problems and to explore possibilities for their solution. While the advisory staff was always accessible for consultation, they also joined the residents of Yambele once every fortnight to continue the educational program, participate in the ongoing evaluation of the process, or confer with the leaders and assist in further planning.

The meetings were held in a building which was the property of the president—formerly a dance hall but now bearing a sign that reads: COMMITTEE FOR THE WELFARE OF YAMBELE. Furnishing this place was one of the first ventures in working together of the inhabitants of Yambele. They gave small contributions for buying the materials, while carpenters volunteered their labor for making large benches to accommodate the people.

The community gave priority to the need for water and electricity and appointed a representative committee to visit the planning board to explore the possibility of extending the public water and electricity facilities to Yambele, even though the community had been illegally established. At the request of the community the student social worker was included in this delegation. During the interview the officers of the planning board made it clear that as long as Yambele continued its growth as a suburban slum it would never receive the public utilities demanded. The residents then held a meeting to discuss the information from the planning board, and the professional team explained what the residents could do in order to have Yambele declared a stationary or arrested slum. All the neighbors promised to watch so that no other clandestine dwellings were built, and they offered to better their own houses to conform to sanitary standards. While the professional team helped to interpret policies and regulations, the neighbors pooled their resources for the building of latrines and the remodeling—in some instances the complete rebuilding—of their homes. After a period of six months the public water and electricity facilities were granted.

The health problems of the community were tackled in various ways. Films depicting common diseases such as ascariasis, gastro-enteritis, and uncinariasis were shown. The medical social workers commented on their social implications. Preventive measures were discussed mainly by the health educator and the sanitary inspector. The nurse stimulated the examination of stools, and treatment was given by the public health physicians to persons suffering from para-sitogenic diseases. By the end of this campaign the consulting team shared the satisfaction of the community at the fact that all the houses had sanitary latrines, the children were not walking barefoot, and the municipal government had agreed to extend its garbage-collection service to Yambele.[2]

You will note that the student caused the ten leaders to come together to consider what to do about the lack of running water and electricity and other community needs. Thus, these ten became the firm central core of citizen enthusiasm (the small, compact center of the snowball in our metaphor). The student then inter-viewed six professional workers in the fields of public health and social work and so brought into being an advisory committee of experts to help the citizens. The third step was to call a mass meeting of all householders. Seventy-five attended the first meeting and many problems were discussed. At a second meeting a formal organization was brought into being called the "Committee for the Welfare of Yambele" with a headquarters building and a board of thirteen officers which continued to meet weekly. Soon at least five of the community needs had been met.

This was a process which any of us might well follow if called upon to serve as a catalyst for community action.

When should one serve as an indirect leader, rather than as the visible leader?

Please note that neither the client nor the social worker (although they initiated the action) were elected to office in the "Committee for the Welfare of Yambele." This is an important point. If you wish to do a good job as a catalyst to start a new organization, do not get yourself elected to office in it. Otherwise this is what may happen:

Colton Community Council, U.S.A.

Miss Fairfax was hired by the Board of Public Welfare of the town of Colton as their first social worker. She was a person of remarkable energy and a good public speaker. Although as a social case worker she was carrying a heavy load, she spent her evenings planning to bring into being a community council for Colton. Although there were only about 5000 inhabitants there were exactly 100 organizations when she included not only the Salvation Army and the Boy and Girl Scouts but the various lunch clubs, the Grange and even the Ancient Order of Hibernians. At Christmas time there was much duplication in the distribution of Christmas baskets to the poorer families. Miss Fairfax had worked with a community council in a larger city and felt that Colton needed one, not only to co-ordinate its present services but to plan for the future.

She decided to act at once by inviting two representatives of each organization to come to a public meeting to discuss the matter. She asked the First Selectman (the New England equivalent of a mayor) to send out the invitations. When he declined, she sent it out herself signing herself as "Town Social Worker." Rather to her surprise the meeting was crowded. The Kiwanians came lest the Rotary Club might get some more favorable publicity. The Women's Club of the Congregational Church attended when they heard that the women of the Methodist Church were going to be represented. The First Selectman consented to preside but merely introduced Miss Fairfax to explain what it was all about. As she faced the audience of nearly 200 people she felt that they must have just been waiting for her to call them together for this needed service. (Actually many came out of curiosity and because Miss Fairfax was new in town and therefore had publicity value.) She was an inspiring speaker and sold the idea well. She introduced a little humor and after a few questions and answers, they accepted the plan, appointed a committee to serve with Miss Fairfax in drafting by-laws and agreed to meet again in a month. Thus the Colton Community Council came to birth with little difficulty and none of the slow preliminaries used by Miss Parker; no convincing Mr. A to speak to Mr. B; no getting a small committee together and no community study.

In fairness to Miss Fairfax it must be admitted that the Council lasted for two years and did several good things including sending a delegation to the legislature to favor some needed social legislation. Miss Fairfax was the secretary of the council and gave vigorous leadership. Then she and a member of her public welfare board disagreed as to the amount of relief she had given to a client. Miss Fairfax was accused of violating the instructions of the board. The majority exonerated her but she had become angry and resigned. The community council which had rested entirely on her shoulders died the moment she got on the train to leave Colton. Some years later I interviewed the postmaster of Colton who had been chairman of the council. When asked whether the community council was still going, he scratched his head in perplexity. "Community Council? Community Council?" he said. When reminded that he had been its chairman, he said at last: "Oh! You mean that thing that Miss Fairfax was interested in."[3]

Perhaps if Miss Fairfax had followed Miss Parker's example in Woodhurst and had slowly built up a small interested group of citizens to help her start the council, they might have carried it on after she left. Then, too, if she wished the organization to last, it would have been far better to have had someone else serve as the secretary and visible leader.

A wise and experienced social worker, George L. Warren, once

distinguished between what he called Direct Leadership and Indirect Leadership as follows:

Warren on "Indirect Leadership"

Direct Leadership requires that the leader stand before the group as
the recognized leader. He has a face-to-face relationship with its
members. His position is obvious and public. He has accepted formal
office and all the glory and acclaim of success or the ignominy and
criticism of failure are to be his. Whether his leadership be autocratic
or democratic, wise or unwise, skillful or ineffective, his responsibility
is fixed and accepted by all.

Indirect leadership lacks the element of recognized responsibility. It
works quietly, behind the scenes, through others. It is skillful in its
choice of direct leaders. It receives neither credit nor blame. It accepts
no formal office. Indirect leadership has broad vision and purpose and
is more lasting in time. Without the power and prestige which attach to
official position, the indirect leader provides inspiration, guidance,
energy, and frequently co-ordination to direct leaders in functional
groups.

Social programs require both direct and indirect leadership for their
fulfillment. Where the harmonious action of diverse groups is required,
the co-operation of the direct leaders of the individual groups is essential. The particular situation or program may or may not require open
direct leadership of the leaders of interested groups. It is unwise and in
fact impractical to generalize here. My main purpose at the moment is
to stress the very real distinction between direct and indirect leadership, and to suggest that each has its particular place in the development of a social program.

The professional social worker is often spoken of as a leader. Is his
position one of direct or indirect leadership? I think we will all recognize that statesmanship requires that he consciously assume an attitude
of indirect leadership. A true leader aims so to organize and develop
his particular effort that when he withdraws those who have been
associated with him in it will have acquired a sense of responsibility
that will carry the effort along with approximately the same effectiveness without him. This is, of course, an ideal which is seldom realized

in practice, and it should be recognized that no one has ever succeeded in organizing any piece of work so effectively that it operates itself. On the other hand it is useful to state this objective as a contrast to the opposite extreme in which an executive, through a failure to appreciate his function of indirect leadership, acquires or attaches to himself so many functions which should be borne by others that the whole effort comes to a sudden stop when he departs.

But there are many other reasons for the assumption of indirect leadership by the professional social worker. Action on any social program is dependent in the first instance on group or community consciousness of need. A leader to be effective must have followers. Followers must be conscious of the purpose in which they are being led. An executive must therefore develop group consciousness and create the desire for action before effective action can result. Once the desire for action is aroused the executive capitalizes the opportunity of the situation to develop a leader in the group rather than accepting direct leadership himself. In this manner a new leader is developed and group action results. Something has been created. The executive is then left free to repeat the process in a different or related direction.

Were the executive to assume direct leadership at this point, his time would be absorbed on one special phase only of his many-sided task. His assumption of direct leadership would attract to him other tasks and he would soon find himself loaded with responsibilities and surrounded by inactive associates. Further, each project has within itself elements of success and failure. Success in this specific effort brings with it prestige which in turn attracts other opportunities and with them the developing danger of being blinded by the will to power. At this point short cuts are taken and the need for co-operative technique is lost sight of. The slow process of developing group consciousness, desire for action, and then action, becomes irksome and the executive soon finds himself out of step with his group.

Failure, too, has its dangers. To have failed in a specific project in which direct leadership and responsibility have been assumed reflects on the executive. The reasons for failure may have been quite beyond his control, but the blame will be placed on the leader. While one or two such failures may be condoned, a succession of them will soon diminish the worker's effectiveness on the job as a whole.

It should be recognized also that direct leaders in any group are always fair target for the opposition of others who aspire to leadership. Unseating the leader is a typical American pastime. The group or crowd is quick to acclaim, but also as quickly shifts its affections and following to the new leader. The operation of crowd psychology is perhaps not as prevalent in the field of social work as in the political field, but we should always be conscious that much the same psychological principles are operating in both fields. I am quite familiar with the details of at least two situations in which direct leadership before the public on certain issues was assumed by executives. Both situations probably justified the assumption of direct leadership, but the usefulness of each executive was definitely limited in time thereafter. I do not say that such direct leadership should never be assumed, but only that it should be consciously done with the definite weighing of immediate gains against the losses in permanent and continuing usefulness.[4]

The late Eduard Lindeman (who was a colleague of mine on the faculty of the New York School of Social Work at Columbia University) used to object to the term "indirect leadership." He said it sounded "kind of sneaky." There should be nothing of timidity or dishonesty about it. It is a sincere technique adopted by a community worker because he has the welfare of the movement at heart and wants to be sure that it will not cease when he leaves the community. His willingness to give others the credit and to have them have the visible leadership is not due to generosity or to modesty. He is interested in building a stronger community and he knows that one way to develop new leaders is to encourage them to accept direct leadership of the movement. George L. Warren (quoted above) once served as vice-president of a civic agency of which I was the executive. When I learned that he was not going to stand for re-election the next year, I expostulated with him. His reply was characteristic. He said: "You know that I will always continue to work for the organization even if I do not hold office. It is time that *this office should be educating someone else*."

Obviously Miss Parker, in Woodhurst, exerted indirect leadership. During the process she remained, as far as possible, invisible. She never sought credit for herself. I looked up the first annual report of the Woodhurst Mental Health Society. Miss Parker's name was never mentioned in it, yet it was she, and she alone, who first set the movement going. For those of us who seek to stimulate and direct community action, indirect leadership is obviously the wisest course: to let others, direct leaders, take the credit and thus make the movement *theirs,* not ours.

In Sarbandan (see Chapter II) Miss Najafi faced a problem similar to that which Miss Fairfax confronted:

Sarbandan (continued)

From the time that I had come to Sarbandan I had tried to get the council to take responsibility for the improvement of the village. They met around my samovar nearly every Thursday afternoon. In October they voted me the secretary of the council. They would have made me chairman but I was not an actual member and, besides, a woman in that position is unheard of in the villages.

Our membership differed from the usual village council in that we had many small landlords and these ordinarily represented themselves on the council. When they voted that something needed to be done I encouraged them to vote also that they would do it as far as possible, by themselves.

. . . . .

As secretary I could make application to any agency of the government in the name of the council. Of course, having lived all my life in Teheran, except for my school years in America, I ordinarily made such applications through personal friends. A much easier way to do things in Iran as well as in other places.

I took my position as secretary seriously and tried to get the council members to take their positions seriously, too. They voted that if a member were absent without cause for three times he no longer belonged to the council. And now belonging to the council was of real importance. It gave status and dignity to both the individuals and the group.

The council voted to invite a representative of Point Four to Sarbandan. I forwarded this invitation. The council presided at the turning of the first earth for the bath. The trouble I had with that bath! . . .

I was making my home neat one morning when Mash'hadi Mokhtar appeared at my door.

"Lady Najafi, it is terrible, terrible."

"What is terrible?"

"Point Four will destroy our bath before the new one is built. We will have no bath!"

. . . . .

"What are you going to do about it, Mashdi Mokhtar?"

"Me? I thought you would do something, Lady Najafi."

"What can I do? I am not really a member of the council. My word does not have weight with Point Four," I said. "Call a meeting of the council at the teahouse. Invite representatives from Point Four to be there. Then explain that we cannot be without a bath and tell them why. They do not understand, perhaps, that a bath is a religious necessity."

"But, my lady, you know how to say these things."

"So do you, Mashdi Mokhtar. So do the others." . . .

"I think you do not know what this means, my lady."

"Believe me, I do understand, Mashdi Mokhtar. You will have to fight for what you want."

I knew that I must not "mix in." I would not be in the village always, perhaps not very long, and the people must have practice in fighting their own battles. . . .

And so the old bath was left while work on the new bath was begun.[5]

It is evident that Miss Najafi could have easily allowed herself to have become as dominant in Sarbandan as Miss Fairfax became in Colton. In determining not to "mix in" and to insist that the villagers must "fight for what they wanted," she was deliberately endeavoring to remain an indirect leader.

An indirect leader engages in a subtle but most effective form of adult education. Here is an example:

Miss Foster and the International Institute, U.S.A.

Many years ago I was engaged to organize and operate a community chest in an industrial New England city. Our population at that time consisted, by less than thirty per cent, of "old Yankee" stock. Sixty-three per cent were foreign born or children of foreign born, yet few of us were conscious of these facts or of their significance. The YWCA operated an International Institute and engaged a Miss Foster as director. Her task was not only to serve the foreign born but to awaken the native born, who still dominated the town, to a consciousness of the fine things in these various cultures.

Miss Foster had none of the physical characteristics which are generally associated with one whose task is to stimulate community action. She was in poor health, nervous, and lacked charm. We generally think of a "community organizer" as a dynamic figure, radiating force and thus compelling others to activity—generally a virile man. Miss Foster was just the opposite, yet she performed her task superbly. She adroitly educated the leaders of our town, from the chief justice of our superior court to the community chest secretary, and after three years she passed on to a bigger job leaving our city better than she found it. Her technique was to get each of us to volunteer to do a job which would educate us. She proposed a hand-craft exhibit to be shown in all the branch libraries exhibiting the beautiful things inherited in the cultures of each of the nineteen different nationalities represented in our city. The announced purpose was to awaken the second-generation foreign born to an appreciation of the fine things in their own inheritance by seeing the native born admiring them. Miss Foster was skilled in planning the mechanics of such an exhibit. I found myself volunteering to call at the home of a Swedish photographer to borrow a beautiful wedding dress which had descended through six generations. My acquaintance with the family had a profound effect upon me. [When I was] a boy in Wisconsin we spoke of Swedes as "square heads." I have never been able to use that disparaging epithet about a Swedish person since.

Next, Miss Foster went to work on the chief justice. When foreign-born residents finished night school in preparation for citizenship, it was the custom perfunctorily to mail to them their graduation certificates. Miss Foster suggested a graduation ceremony. The chief justice agreed to hand out the diplomas. More important than the ceremony itself was his experience in heading a representative committee to plan the details of the ceremony. On this committee the chief justice became associated with the leading Hungarian priest and the leading Polish surgeon. These three leaders came to know and respect each other as men apart from their cultural backgrounds. The unity of these three had a profound effect on future events in our town.

Her final project was a Spring Festival in which ten different nationalities portrayed the traditional songs and dances by which all peoples celebrate the coming of spring. This filled the largest auditorium in town for three nights with one of the most artistic performances the city had ever experienced. However, Miss Foster also had an ulterior purpose. Preparation for the affair required activity by committees and subcommittees. Hundreds of us were involved. Some worked backstage changing scenery, climbed stepladders and ran errands. Becoming thus involved, we obtained a new appreciation of the contributions which our immigrants make to America. In recent years I have met (in New York and in Washington at meetings to promote more intelligent immigration laws) persons with whom I worked backstage at the Spring Festival. Miss Foster's indirect leadership was still impelling them to action.[6]

What are the dangers of too much pressure, and when should the worker advise delay?

There is an old story about an ancient Ford car blocking traffic on Fifth Avenue in New York. It was the rush hour in the afternoon, and chauffeurs and taxicab drivers were blowing their horns with impatience. Again and again the old Ford would start up only to stop again. As it moved to the corner of Forty-second street, the traffic policeman yelled, "Come on! Come on! Can't you go any faster?" The driver of the Ford leaned out of the window and replied sadly, "*I* could but I don't like to leave my car."

In a democracy *community progress cannot proceed any faster than the understanding and consent of the majority of the citizens.* Small energized groups can initiate community action and conduct effective demonstrations of needed progress, but if official action becomes necessary a large segment of the population must be awakened. It is a condition which we must accept with our faith in democracy. Bernard Shaw said: "What the public is not *up* on, they are likely to be *down* on." Only in an autocracy can social or civic change happen rapidly without "the consent of the governed." If many are to join the cause enthusiastically so that it becomes a movement "by the people" as well as "for the people," the best way is to get many citizens *involved* in it. The arts of advertising and publicity are not enough. Citizens must be more intimately associated with the movement if it is to become *theirs* so that they in turn influence others.

Sometimes it is even wise to endeavor to hold back the more enthusiastic members of the community to give time for others to catch up and become involved. For instance:

Barrio Cuyon, Puerto Rico

In Puerto Rico in April, 1951, Zacarius Rodriguez, a field organizer for the Division of Community Education, first visited Barrio Cuyon. This was a small rural village bisected by a river which occasionally overflowed its banks so that the teachers could not cross the river to the school. He visited several homes on both sides of the river and found that no doctor had ever visited the Barrio. They talked of health problems and the need of a medical center and milk station for children. Rodriguez arranged to return and show a motion picture of how another barrio had constructed such a milk station and medical center by the voluntary labor of its citizens. Rodriguez paid fourteen successive visits to the barrio and talked with most of the villagers. Seven different meetings were held to discuss the matter. The location of the center (on which side of the river) had to be agreed upon. At the end of a year of visiting and discussing, the organizer was still reminding the villagers "that we will have to meet many more times to reach conclusions since the *ideas of everybody are necessary for a matter* which concerns everybody." Five months later the villagers were at work constructing the building.[7]

The growing strength of united community fund campaigns throughout the United States is due not only to the sound policy of substituting one united campaign for many competitive ones. It is also due to the vast number of citizens who volunteer to take an active part in these campaigns. Even in a small city, 500 team workers is not an unusual number. They solicit each other and strive to compete with each other to win the announced goal. They (with their families, neighbors, and friends) exert a powerful influence on public opinion.

However, such a general upsurge of public opinion by *involving* many citizens must be brought about slowly, wisely, and without undue pressure.

Eastford United Fund, U.S.A.

In the city of Eastford, John Blackmore contracted to bring such a campaign into being within three months. His was a most dynamic personality. He believed in the crude use of financial and social pressure. Social agencies that were unwilling to join the united campaign were dragooned into it by pressure from bank presidents and employers who had strong influence over members of the boards of the agencies. In the campaign similar "strong arm" methods were used to compel citizens and groups of employees to give to the campaign. Public announcement was finally made that the goal had been approximately reached. Mr. Blackmore collected his fee and left town to try his pressure methods elsewhere.

However, many of the campaign pledges proved uncollectible. The member agencies never received the full amounts budgeted to them. Pressure methods used on employee groups resulted in an adverse reaction and bitter resentment. Before a year was out the united plan had failed and Medford returned to costly and ineffective competitive campaigns.[8]

You may remember that in Suh Kam Chon (Chapter II above) Glen Leet even cautioned against insisting that every citizen should volunteer to take part in the work because, he said, "the workers know from experience that whenever there is 100 per cent participation there is at least some social pressure and therefore such work is not entirely voluntary." Here is an example of enthusiasm spoiled by too much pressure:

El Manayel, Egypt

The small village of El Manayel, fifteen miles northeast of Cairo, was chosen by the Egyptian Association for Social Studies for an experiment to discover the best techniques for raising the standard of living in an Egyptian village. Mohammed Shalaby, a student at the Cairo School of Social Work, was chosen to live in the village and operate a social center there. One evening some of the fathers gathered at the center were complaining about being fined for their children's absences from school. These children were supposed to go to the nearest school which was in a distant village, but the children played on their way to school and in many cases did not reach the school or attend the classes. A father in such a case was responsible and was liable to a fine of from P.T. 15 to P.T. 100 (sixty cents to four dollars). Such a fine at that time represented two or three days' wages. A discussion started concerning the injustice of these rules and directed attention to the need for a school in their own village.

The people assembled on succeeding evenings, continuing their discussion until they decided to send a petition to the officials in charge of education at Cairo asking for a school for El Manayel and expressing their willingness to give any help within their power to achieve this purpose.

A few days later a petition was signed by nearly every father in the village. Most of the signatures were thumbprints of petitioners with the name of each written under his mark. This petition was presented to the officials in Cairo who immediately communicated with the governor of the province, who had been previously informed about the project and had become interested in this particular problem and the discussion around it. He agreed to establish a school at El Manayel, allocating a certain sum of money for the building and an annual budget, if the people would provide the site.

The people were more than willing, but where? Every square foot of the land was cultivated intensively and worth good money, or was occupied by a house or street. They were at a loss until Mohammed Shalaby offered a suggestion. There was a pond at the village entrance, covering one and one-third *feddans*. If this pond were filled in, it would be the most suitable site for a school. As this area of the Egyptian Delta is flat, there was nothing to put into the pond. However, if the village streets were leveled, the earth and rubbish removed might fill the pond. This would not only provide a site for the school but would improve the streets and eliminate one of the chief breeders of disease in the village. The idea was considered and adopted, and the work started on a co-operative basis outlined by a committee composed of some elder villagers who assumed responsibility for the job. The work moved slowly.

Some weeks later the governor, concerned about the slow progress, *ordered the police officer of the district to make the people finish filling the pond at once.* Ten uniformed policemen and their officer came to the village to carry out the order of the governor. The people were brought from their fields with their donkeys and camels and were obliged to transport anything in sight to the edge of the water, including their stored fuel (cotton and cornstalks).

Shalaby was not in El Manayel that morning. When he returned at noon, there was a great outcry among the villagers and anger on their faces. He immediately phoned the governor. An order was given to the policemen to withdraw, but not until much damage had been done to the experiment. The people were disappointed, and Mohammed Shalaby's position in the village was seriously impaired.

It was difficult to restore the confidence and interest of the people but, little by little, some results were achieved. The governor came to understand that the voluntary method of doing the project was of more concern to the people than the pond, as such, and that his method of trying to help was not the right one. He offered El Manayel a truck for a few days to transport soil from a nearby spot on the Ismailia Canal to the edge of the pond where the people leveled it off at their convenience. The road from the main highway to the village was narrow and not suitable for the truck, so the people widened it. The work progressed and in a few weeks there was a site for the school. To the great satisfaction of the people an excellent building was erected and the school started within fifteen months of the beginning of the experiment.[9]

Obviously sending the police to make the people work faster tended to spoil the whole spirit of the enterprise. Only after great difficulty was this spirit re-established.

How can the school serve as a catalyst?

It is evident from this Egyptian experience (and from many others like the Mexican and East Indian illustrations in Chapter III above) that the need for a school is one of the first "felt needs" of many communities in different countries. Here are two further illustrations:

Sutlej Valley, Pakistan

And so I found myself sitting in the mud-walled village of 211/9R —the name indicates its location in the Sutlej Valley irrigation project—about four miles from the nearest road. I was about to hear youngsters who had never seen an Englishman or an American read to me in English. . . .

Seven years ago there was no school here. Today sixty-five children, nineteen of them girls, attend classes every morning except on Fridays. The school itself, a thatched, mud-walled hut located at one end of a mud-floored courtyard, had neither desks nor chairs. It did have a blackboard made by the village carpenter. Like the blackboards in most of America's early one-room schools, this consisted of wooden boards painted black. But it worked, and it was used.

Next year the thatched mud hut will be replaced by a brick building the men of the village were constructing themselves.

"It will cost us about 2000 rupees," one of them said to me, "but it will be as good as a 10,000 rupee government school." He may very well have been right, too, for the villagers do not count the value of the gifts they receive toward the building of their school—such as all the palm tree trunks used for beams.

. . . . .

This school at 211/9R, as fine an example of civic pride as one could hope to see, had been started largely with village initiative, and was administered by the local school board.[10]

Pei-Yeh, Taiwan

At Pei-Yeh Primary School in a poverty-stricken mountainous region, the parents contributed their labor to construct buildings and to dig out a fine playground on the side of the mountain.[11]

One such successful experience (as we discovered in Chapter III) usually sets up a chain-reaction encouraging the citizens to embark on further self-help projects. Thus the building of a school, itself, acts as a catalyzing experience, spurring the people on to further community action. However, in many communities the building of the school has been followed by the arrival of an educational leader who proved to be not only a teacher but a catalyst as well:

Galino, Iran

Three years ago . . . Mr. Shahrifzadeh (the worker responsible for training teachers) helped 400 people of Galino construct a good school building. The boys came from six nearby villages. The Public Health Department helped dig a well over 120 feet deep and install a pump. The Fundamental Education Worker, Mr. Ameli, has worked three years in Galino. Eight per cent of the homes have installed sanitary toilets. Mr. Shahrifzadeh and Mr. Ameli helped settle a long-standing dispute with a nearby village over distribution of water. They induced men of both villages to co-operate in building a new surface canal system to separate the water at the river source and bring the rightful amount to each village.[12]

Here is a similar example of the school as a catalyst for community action:

Deh Shin, Taiwan

The Tung-Shih Community School has adopted a demonstration village. Dr. E. E. Neal, a visiting consultant, visited Deh Shin, the experimental village. He asked the village leader why for the twenty-three years he had lived in the village (most of them as village chief) he had not sought the assistance of . . . the school. He replied: "Ours is a very poor village. . . . I thought of the school as only concerned with teaching books and not interested in community problems. I was ashamed to approach any of the agencies, but when the school people came to us to discuss our problems with us, that was different. I knew I could get assistance for improving our village." There was no approach road. Now one can drive all the way up to the village. Neal saw newly constructed village streets, newly installed hand pumps, each house connected with electricity. Electricity was what the people wanted most. The school helped the people organize and collect enough money to pay for the installation. The hogs had been taken out of the lanes and put in pens; the wells had been improved and compost pits dug. Neal asked how much money the school had contributed to get these things done. The village leader said, "None. All these activities were the people's own efforts. . . . You have seen the streets, hand pumps, electricity, etc., but the real contribution is intangible. It is a spirit of co-operation and a feeling of importance." Asked as to future plans, he said, "We plan to build a community center for the education of the people. It will take too long to educate the people by going from house to house." The center is now becoming a reality with some assistance from the township government.[13]

An interesting experience of co-operation between school and community is reported from The Philippines:

Urdaneta, Philippines

The ordinance against loose pigs and other animals was not being enforced. The policeman was paid by contributions of rice at the harvest season, "No mercy on pigs, no rice" was the custom which had grown up. The Bactad Elementary School appointed two squads of special "catchers of stray pigs." They were older boys supervised by a male teacher appointed by the mayor of Urdaneta. All the other pupils acted as "informants" or "intelligence observers" reporting that a pig, goat, buffalo, or horse was loose. The squad would then catch the animal. The owner would be asked to read the ordinance and to promise not to let it loose again. If the owner could not build a pen, the squad would build it. All who wished might co-operate, and it became a community affair. No second offense occurred. The pupils calculated the amount of loss due to destruction by the animal, and the owner was shown the value of the manure from the animals penned up.

Also 105 male high school students and 7 male teachers built a dam and raised dykes which led water to the Urdaneta high school grounds.[14]

*   *   *

Summary. The community worker serves as a catalyst. He exerts indirect leadership. The volunteer community leaders should get the credit and assume the responsibility for the community action. The movement may start by a few representative citizens being brought together to consider the need and plans to meet it. They thus become a nucleus of common interest steadily attracting more and more citizens into the movement. It is well to make haste slowly and avoid too much pressure or the use of force. The school can serve as an effective catalyst for community action.

V. SPECIALISTS

How can the community worker serve as a channel through which the technical knowledge of experts can be co-ordinated and made available to the local community?

Thor Heyerdahl believed that the ancestors of the Polynesians might have come from South America. (Eventually he proved that this was possible by building a balsa-wood raft named Kon-Tiki on which he and his companions drifted with the trade winds across the Pacific.) His original idea he embodied in a manuscript entitled: "Polynesia and America: a Study of Prehistoric Relations." He presented this to eminent anthropologists, archeologists, and other scientists. None of them would even read it. One friend, an ethnologist, explained:

Kon-Tiki and the Specialists

All the people you've been to see think it's just a passing idea you've got. . . . [It's] your way of approaching the problem. They're specialists, the whole lot of them, and they don't believe in a method of work which cuts into every field of science from botany to archeology. They limit their own scope in order to be able to dig in the depths with more concentration for details. Modern research demands that every special branch shall dig in its own hole. It's not usual for anyone to sort out what comes up out of the holes and try to put it all together.[1]

One of the most important jobs of a local community worker is this "putting together" of advice from many specialists (sometimes conflicting) so as to make it useful to his community—for example:

Beechmont Community Council, U.S.A.

In Beechmont, George Hallworthy's job as executive of the Council is to co-ordinate the work of some forty public and private departments and agencies specializing in health and welfare services. He also bears the prime responsibility for stimulating and leading them to plan jointly for improved services to the growing community in the future. His social work training included what is known as social casework, social group work and community organization. He is not expert in the technical fields of housing, public health, adult education and public administration, and other technical areas involved in such social planning for the future of Beechmont. However, he is skilled at organizing committee meetings and larger community meetings to receive and discuss technical advice received from state departments and national health and welfare agencies.

Before community councils came into being in the United States in the 1920s and 1930s each national agency approached Beechmont in a competitive manner. The national health agencies, recreation agencies, or family agencies each promoted its specialty in Beechmont. As someone said, each tried to put its agency on the map and didn't care what happened to the map. Soon Beechmont was spending more per capita for public health nursing than any city in the country, while her delinquency rate among youths, and the number of children injured in street accidents for lack of adequate playgrounds mounted alarmingly. Today these experts at the national and state level serve Beechmont in a co-ordinated manner through Hallworthy and the Community Council.[2]

Here is an example from Jordan of the need for advice from many specialists and the problem of co-ordinating it:

Olive Trees in Jordan

The basic problem in many villages was how to rejuvenate the olive trees. Having established the problem, it was then necessary for the community development worker to find (a) a soil specialist; (b) an irrigation man; (c) an agricultural expert; and (d) a plant man. Once a group decision had been reached it was necessary to bridge the gap between these co-ordinated technicians and the people of the village.[3]

About 1953 the new government of Indonesia found itself facing competition among specialists, such as has plagued many older nations. The Ministry of Agriculture proposed to establish various agricultural centers in the island of Java to demonstrate improved methods of farming. The Ministry of Health, quite independently, was planning health centers throughout Java, and the Ministry of Education had distinct plans for centers of adult education to combat illiteracy. There was no co-ordination among these plans although the war against the three allies of ignorance, starvation, and disease is one united struggle which can be won only by attacking all three fronts at once. Starving people cannot learn. Sick people cannot embrace new methods of farming. People who cannot read are seriously handicapped in learning how to keep well and adapt modern agricultural methods.

Even on the international level there was no co-ordination. The three ministers in Indonesia received separate support from the specialized units of the United Nations. UNESCO (United Nations Economic, Scientific, and Cultural Organization) backed up the Ministry of Education in its plans for separate adult education centers. FAO (Food and Agricultural Organization) similarly supported the Minister of Agriculture, and WHO (World Health Organization) gave effective support to the Ministry of Health in its plans for separate health centers. The new nation obviously could not afford separate centers for each specialty, nor would such separate and financially competitive efforts have been the most effective way to serve the people of Java.

About the same time the government of Thailand was experimenting with a so-called "pilot project" which was ideal from the standpoint of co-ordination of all departments and all specialties, national and international, but which made no provision for participation by the local villagers.

Bang Pa Kong, Thailand

The Bang Pa Kong community development project was established in July, 1952, in Chachoengsao Province, sixty kilometers south of Bangkok. It was transformed from one of the eight "self-help settlements" which the Thai Government through its Minister of the Interior organized (about 1943) to provide landless people with salt land along the Gulf of Thailand for reclamation and cultivation. The government built a long dike to shut out the salt water, and dug canals to provide fresh water from the river to wash and to irrigate the land. Governmental loans were made available to the settlers to build houses and to purchase implements, animals, windmills and other necessary equipment. The settlers also received loans at an annual interest of 5 per cent to meet family expenses until the first crop was harvested.

The settlement at Bang Pa Kong has 2,709 *rai* (25 *rai* equals one acre) of land, allotted to eighty-five families, comprising 600 people. A recent report states that 1,951 *rai* have been cleared and are under cultivation. The size of farms varies from twenty-five to seventy-five *rai* according to the location of the land and the size of a settler's family. The average farm is thirty *rai*. The settlers reside in five different neighborhoods.

The fundamental education pilot project organized by the Thai government in co-operation with the United Nations Educational, Scientific, and Cultural Organization and the United States Mutual Security Agency, is situated in Chachoengsao, sixty kilometers from the Bang Pa Kong community development project, which thus has not only the benefit of the settlement's groundwork but also the advantage of using the facilities of this pilot project. These appear to be the reasons why Bang Pa Kong was selected as the site of the community development project.

A "Statement of Policy" adopted by the Bang Pa Kong community development committee at its first meeting in July, 1952 declared that it planned to develop the colony "into a model rural community in all aspects of life: economic, social, cultural, educational, physical as well as spiritual, for demonstration and training purposes. Since life is a whole the improvement of one (aspect) cannot be very satisfactorily accomplished without the improvement of others." Secondary purposes were listed as follows:

1. To develop competent agricultural and rural leadership.
2. To encourage the colony farmers to improve home and farmstead surroundings.
3. To participate in worthy undertakings for the improvement of agriculture in the colony.
4. To encourage colony farmers in the development of individual farming programs.
5. To develop character, train for useful citizenship, and foster patriotism.
6. To participate in co-operative enterprises.
7. To build the confidence of farm boys and girls and young men and women in themselves and their work.
8. To get settlers out of debt and encourage the practice of thrift.
9. To encourage improvement in education through schools and home efforts.

The statement also declared that the guiding principle in all these activities should be self-help:

"One should never try to work for people but rather work with them. It is through their own organizations that the farmers are trained, and local leadership is developed. No program should ever be imposed on the people. The ultimate goal of the community development is to bring about better farms, better homes, and a better community by the people themselves, through the realization of their own strength and making use of whatever services they can obtain from the government."4

These are fine words. You and I could hardly improve upon them as a statement of general principles of community development. Let us see to what extent these principles were lived up to in practice:

The interesting feature of this experiment is the extent to which international and national agencies appear to have been drawn together to participate in joint planning through representation at monthly meetings of this community development committee, which consisted of seven members, as follows:

One from the Ministry of Interior (Director-General of Department of Public Welfare)

One from the Ministry of Education (Adult Education Officer)

One from the Ministry of Agriculture (Chief of Extension Division)

One from the Mutual Security Agency (Extension Co-ordinator)

One from the United Nations Educational, Scientific, and Cultural Organization (Adult Education Specialist)

Two from the Food and Agriculture Organization (Extension specialist for the region and Agricultural Officer).

The chairman is the director-general of the Department of Public Welfare. The regional agricultural officer (FAO) serves as secretary. The chief of the Bang Pa Kong colonization project (under the Department of Public Welfare) attends each monthly meeting, although he is not a voting member of the committee. The voting members frequently bring with them two or three other staff members from their organizations, who have special interest in or information concerning matters on the agenda.

Representatives of other national and international agencies concerned (such as the Department of Irrigation, Ministry of Co-operatives, Ministry of Public Health, International Labor Organization, World Health Organization, United Nations International Children's Emergency Fund, and the Regional Officer of the United Nations Technical Assistance Administration) have been invited to the meetings of the committee from time to time.5

Thailand is to be congratulated on assembling on one active, planning committee all the national, provincial, and even international agencies whose efforts could benefit Bang Pa Kong. Many nations do not have machinery for co-ordinating and integrating all such forces. Even the various units of the United Nations (such as UNESCO, FAO, WHO, and so forth) may find themselves in some countries backing a particular government department in its specialized work, in competition with the specialists in other departments, and without adequate machinery for co-ordinating such efforts.

However, such a committee, concentrating all its abilities on a settlement of eighty-five families, seems top-heavy. Such a national committee might co-ordinate community development work in many provinces. There might also be a need for provincial committees supervising the operations of community development plans in the villages. Certainly a local committee for one village or a group of villages should have local leaders participating in its work, if maximum, permanent results are to be achieved.

In September, 1952, it was proposed that the community development committee take steps to organize a formal settlers' association. Presumably this would enable the settlers to participate in further planning. A subcommittee of three was appointed to study the proposal. In October, 1952, they submitted this report, which to you and me must appear surprising:

The original thinking that a formal, financially responsible association be formed appears to this committee to be unworkable at the present time, since it is based on premises of farmers' interest and abilities which are probably entirely outside their experience and tradition. . . . The first step should be to work with the five neighborhood groups into which the colony is naturally divided. Local meetings of the farmers should be held to discuss their problems and needs and to select a leader to represent them on a Central Committee. A Central Settlers Committee of five may be formed from the representatives of the local groups. The Supervisor of the Colony will need to train these officers in the performance of their duties. The Colony Supervisor and the FAO Extension Specialist, and the Changwad (provincial) agricultural and education officers when available should attend the committee meetings as advisors, but care should be taken not to dominate the meetings by their numbers or authority.

The formation and operation of a voluntary organization expressing the desires of the members is probably a *considerable departure from century-old custom and tradition in Thailand. Farm people have for generations expected the government to do things for them, and the Bang Pa Kong Colony has been operated so far on this basis. Thus, the colonists doubtless have little concept of doing things for themselves or the community through activity in a voluntary self-help membership association.*[6] [The italics are mine.]

The defeatist attitude indicated by the words I have italicized would seem to negate the principles stated in the excellent "Statement of Policy" quoted above. Though it is undoubtedly true that "voluntary self-help" would be a "considerable departure from century-old custom," are we to assume that the villagers of Thailand are so inferior to those of the other countries we have studied so far in this book that they could not be led to help themselves as have villagers in Korea, Iran, India, Mexico, Kenya, Ghana, Puerto Rico, Egypt, The Philippines, and Taiwan?

The report of the United Nations from which I have been quoting states that in 1953 the project was "still in the formative stage"—too early to evaluate it. It, however, must be evident to you and me that Bang Pa Kong could not be termed a "pilot project" or demonstration to show other villages what they could do for themselves. On the one hand, it would be preposterous to expect other Thailand villages to be provided with such a high-powered national and international Community Development Committee to assist them paternalistically. On the other hand, Bang Pa Kong is handicapped by not being a normal village. It was artificially created. There is no traditional village government, no headman or Puyaiban, elected by the people. There is not even a local Buddhist *wat* (temple), which in most villages serves as a community meeting place, as well as a center for social and religious activities.

From our standpoint the study of Bang Pa Kong has only two advantages: it presents an example of how national and international agencies may be co-ordinated through their representatives serving on a joint-planning committee. It would also seem to be a glaring example of what not to do in community development.

Some national plans for community development provide for a team of specialists to make a joint study of a village and prescribe for its needs. There are four main objections to this plan. It is, of course, very expensive in time and money. In the second place, it is a new experience for such experts to work in a team and endeavor to see the community whole. Each has been used to "digging in his own hole," as termed in *Kon-Tiki*. They may not agree. One of them must be chairman of the team consisting perhaps of an agriculturist, a public health expert, an educator, an anthropologist, and a social worker. The chairman may tend to overweight the plan with his point of view. In the third place, such a team-study makes little or no provision for including those who are to be helped. For reasons explained above in Chapter III, the co-operation of the citizens in carrying out the plan will probably be lacking. Finally, few such experts possess the "social skills" (see Chapter I above) to win the co-operation of citizens. Working with people is a special art in itself. Relatively few technical experts have this skill or (if they once had it) perhaps they have lost it as the habit of talking down to others, and supervising their work has grown upon them. Our technical schools are so immersed in imparting technical information that few of them give training in the difficult art of getting the community to accept such technical advice. Even a social worker may not be too proficient in this skill unless he has had special training and experience in community organization.

There is a story of a famous oculist who devoted his life to producing a perfect eye. At last he succeeded. His laboratory experiments had resulted in an orb even better than the human eye. Unfortunately death called him while he was still trying to determine how to connect this perfect eye with the optic nerve.

Our technical experts *know* enough now to revolutionize human life and make it vastly better. What they do not know is how to connect this knowledge with the community nerve. This is the job of the community worker. He should not pose as an expert in public health or agriculture or education, but as a facilitator or an enabler, a channel through which the knowledge of the experts, who reinforce him, can flow into the community and be accepted by the people. Passing thus through a single channel, technical advice from a team of experts is co-ordinated and translated in terms which the average citizen can understand and accept.

What are the advantages of a multipurpose community worker?

In 1946, at the request of Prime Minister Nehru, Albert Mayer, a town planner from New York City, came to India to establish a Pilot Project for village planning and reconstruction at Etawah in the state of Uttah Pradesh. Ten years later the Home Minister of the Government of India thus described the plan:

Pilot Project, India

The Pilot Development Project worked out with the assistance of Mr. Mayer was launched in the Etawah district in October, 1948. It was a new experiment in rural planning, under which the task of seeking a better life and of reconstructing and rehabilitating the village was to be undertaken essentially by the villagers themselves. Provision had of course to be made for *expert advice* [the italics are mine] also being available in *technical matters,* but the distinguishing feature of the arrangement was that there was an *integrated scheme,* in which the technical workers functioned as a part of the *over-all village* team, with a feeling of deep interest and participation, so as to invoke and retain the confidence of the village community. Another new idea that was introduced was that of the *multipurpose worker* at the village level. Experience had shown that if villagers were approached by separate functionaries of different nation-building departments, the advice that these offered for the improvement of agriculture through the introduction of better implements, new manuring devices, and high-quality seed, animal husbandry, sanitation, and public health, seldom went home, and showed little practical result. But if these functions in the initial stage were entrusted to a trained individual who was actuated by a genuine spirit of service, the villagers would respond to his advice and draw real benefit from it.[7]

In India the multipurpose village-level worker (sometimes called the Gram Sevak) serves a small circle of villages. His task was thus described by Albert Mayer:

Gram Sevak, India

At the village level, advice and help in agriculture, animal husbandry, and public health are not very technical. It has been found that one worker, *backed by available personnel at a higher technical level* [the italics are mine], can do agricultural demonstrations (varietal, manurial, and implemental), animal husbandry inoculations and human vaccinations, help insect control and antimalaria work, and help to organize simple public works by the people, such as lane widening, drainage, and compost pits. Not only can he be trained in this simple work, but his training also includes methods of village approach— group meetings, individual discussions, popular songs, and simple dramas—in short, social education. He can use this approach and the friendliness and friendships that flow from it to introduce work and practices not only in one branch, but in several branches of village life and need.

Being "multipurpose," that is, filling many needs at his level, covering the work of several departments, he needs to cover fewer villages. In other words, he visits and works in the villages of his circle frequently enough so that he becomes well known and well received. Where this new system has been tried, it has been found that four to six villages per man can be well covered. He *can* become a close and trusted adviser, helper, energizer participant.[8]

The Indian plan called for a team of four or five technical advisers (in such subjects as agriculture, public health, education, and so forth) to serve a block of 100 villages and act as technical aids to the village-level workers.

A somewhat similar plan is in operation under the Near East Foundation in an area in Iran. Here thirty village level workers cover 150 villages. Acting as a connecting link between various technicians and the villagers they helped to bring about the following changes:

Varamin Plains, Iran

1. New methods of spraying wheat, melons, cucumbers, and cotton against pests.
2. New varieties of crops and seeds; introduced dooryard gardens.
3. Distributed hatching eggs and carried out a chicken exchange program of Iranian cockerels for American New Hampshires.
4. Livestock selection and spraying of barns and artificial insemination for improving dairy cows.
5. Helped organize rural co-operatives.
6. Introduced sanitary practices.
7. Helped organize self-help projects for improving schools, roads, bridges, mosques, and baths.
8. Taught or organized literacy classes.[9]

Some specialists criticize this use of a "generalist" or multipurpose worker. They fear that he may try to be a jack-of-all-trades and not call in the specialists when he should. Here is one example:

Soybeans in Pakistan

A village level worker in a Pakistan village had received some instruction in nutrition. He was sure that the village people needed more protein, and knew that this could be supplied by soybeans. He therefore procured some seed. He saw no reason for calling in an agriculturalist to give instructions as to planting and cultivation, and probably wished to have the sole credit for the enterprise. The farmers received no instructions, and received practically no yield. Next year they asked for different seed. He should have called in, or at any rate consulted, an agriculturalist.[10]

Both Miss Najafi in Sarbandan, Iran, and Mr. Wiser in Karimpur, India (see Chapter II above) found it difficult to explain to the villagers that although they, as workers, were competent to give first aid, they must consult a doctor on more serious matters. They stuck strictly to this policy and never yielded to the temptation to go beyond their competence. If the multipurpose worker is well trained to understand his own limitations and is conscientious about calling in specialists when he should, there need be no danger in following the plan which seems to be working so well in India. Indeed, he should become less multipurpose and more a bridge between the experts and the villagers.

*   *   *

Summary. The solution of a community's various problems requires the combined help of experts in many fields of specialized knowledge. It is seldom feasible for a team or committee of these specialists to visit the community and give their combined advice. Few specialists have the time or the skill to stimulate the community to accept and act on such advice. The best solution seems to be a well-trained multipurpose worker resident in the community to serve as a catalyst and a channel through which the knowledge of various specialists may be co-ordinated and made available to the community. It is highly important that such a worker should clearly understand the limits of his competence, and when to call in a specialist.

VI.   COMMITTEES

What is the importance of the committee in community action?

You will remember that de Tocqueville (see Chapter I) discovered that community action in America began with the formation of a committee. There is an erroneous belief that the committee is a phenomenon peculiar to the United States. Nothing could be further from the truth. Committees exist in all cultures. In almost every case cited in this book there was a committee; if not a formal one, at least an informal one which served the same purpose. *Voluntary* committees are peculiar to *democratic* nations. Dictatorships use committees also, but they must be official so that they can be kept under control. De Tocqueville was accustomed to the Napoleonic police state. Hence his astonishment that in America a committee could be brought into existence "by private citizens on their own initiative" and "without reference to any bureaucrat."

The astonishing thing to me is not that committees are so prevalent in democratic cultures, but that so little careful thought is given as to why and how a committee should be formed. In initiating community action the first use of the committee is to serve as that central "snowball" (see Woodhurst, Chapter IV) or "community of interest." The nucleus of a new organism is capable of gradually attracting more people into the movement and promoting permanent growth. As the movement grows, the initial committee may need to be modified and enlarged to meet many other needs, some of which may be listed as follows:

1. To start the movement (just mentioned above).
2. To plan and decide policies.
3. To represent various groups in the community.
4. To build unity and co-ordinate various groups.
5. To give sponsorship and prestige to the work.
6. To give continuity to the work.
7. To interpret the work to the community.
8. To choose and supervise a paid staff (if one is to be employed).
9. To raise money (if necessary).
10. To interpret the community to the staff member (if one is employed).

When Miss Parker, acting as a catalyst, started the mental health movement in Woodhurst (see Chapter IV) the initial committee which came into existence was as follows:

Woodhurst Mental Health Society, U.S.A. (continued)

Mr Platt, vice-president of the largest manufacturing company in town. On the board of the family service agency and of the YMCA. Interested in mental health because of a mental or nervous handicap from which a member of his family had suffered.

Mrs. Fiske, vice-chairman of the Visiting Nurse Association. Wife of one of the most prominent lawyers. Interested in mental health by a series of lectures given many years before by Clifford Beers, author of *The Mind That Found Itself,* before the Woman's Club.

Mrs. Wardwell, wife of a successful inventor who suffered from physical and nervous handicaps. She is on the board of the State

Society for Mental Health. She was in the group who heard Clifford Beers.

Mrs Byard, a wealthy young widow. On the VNA board. Was in the group that heard Clifford Beers.

Mr. Murphy, employment manager of one of the largest factories, a former social worker. Came to Woodhurst as secretary of the family service agency, of which he became vice-chairman. . . .

Mr Heath, superintendent of schools. Progressive and vigorous. Under a conservative school board. Intensely interested in plans for ungraded classes for children with mental handicaps.

Dr. Wallace, a young neurologist. Interested in psychiatry, in which he is taking courses in a nearby city, and assisting in a mental health clinic. He is secretary of Woodhurst Medical Society and very popular among the doctors.[1]

This initial group hoped to start a clinic. Dr. Wallace would volunteer his services (part time) as soon as he was qualified as a psychiatrist, and the board hoped to employ a trained psychiatric social worker to help him. At the beginning, however, they could care for only a few patients as a demonstration. They conceived their chief job to be interpreting the work to the community (Number 7 above).

Woodhurst was a heterogeneous community with a large Jewish population, many Italian people, and some nineteen other nationality groups. The board was fortunate in securing as an additional member a very intelligent Jewish woman who had formerly had much experience in social work in the city of Cleveland. She was the wife of a prominent trial lawyer.

They were not so fortunate in their choice of an Italian representative. They invited a young Italian attorney. He came to a few meetings but showed little interest. He was running for election to the State Legislature. As soon as he was elected he resigned from the board. Evidently his membership had been only a step to political preferment. The board wished to represent a cross section of the population, but thereafter they thought more of the intelligence and potential interest and enthusiasm of prospective board members than of just what section of the population they represented.

They limited the total membership to twenty-four, feeling that if the board were much larger each member would feel less responsibility and interest. It was argued that if the board became very large, a small executive committee could be elected to do most of the work. Another Woodhurst agency had followed this course, but it was pointed out that the executive committee soon became the real board, and the other members became merely "window dressing" and, being inactive, lost interest in the work.

Another agency in Woodhurst had a board consisting entirely of old people. They went through the form of an annual election; but no one ever resigned and all wished to be re-elected, so no new blood was added to the board. To avoid this the Mental Health Society provided that each member should be elected for three years and then could be re-elected only once. When Mr. Platt, who was chairman, had served for six years, other members of the board wished to amend the by-laws so that he could continue, but he answered as did Mr. Warren (see Chapter IV above) that the position "ought to be educating someone else." Serving on a committee is in fact one of the most effective methods of adult education.

How do we organize a committee for community action?

Here is an example from a village in the Netherlands:

North West Veluwe, Netherlands

The area is a part of the province of Gelderland, and lies on the south coast of the Zuyder Zee between the towns of Amersfort and Zwolle. Its length comes to 70 km. and its width to 15 km. There are about a hundred thousand inhabitants. The majority of them (68 per cent) belongs to the Dutch Reformed Church. Only 4 per cent is Roman Catholic and the rest belongs to several other Protestant churches. The population is known as being very religious.

. . . . .

A hundred years ago the larger part of the population obtained their living from fishing and agriculture. Since then the population has increased considerably through natural growth, and only 34 per cent of the working male population is now employed in agriculture. Fishing has almost disappeared as a result of the reclamation of large parts of the Zuyder Zee. 35 per cent of the working male population is now employed in handicrafts and industry. The North West Veluwe has become a major recreation area, and the letting of rooms to people on holiday is now an important source of income to many. Even so the economic condition of the North West Veluwe is by no means healthy.

. . . . .

The "Foundation for the Development of the North West Veluwe" . . . has been created by the provincial government of Gelderland with the aim of helping the people of the North West Veluwe in finding their own solution to the many problems they are faced with. . . . The Foundation is an autonomous body with its own executive. It is financed from contributions by the national government, the provincial government, and the municipalities. A staff of eight persons is employed on a full-time basis: an agricultural expert, an economist, a social worker, a sociologist, and an administrative staff of four. . . .

Hardly a person can be found who can be regarded as a leader for the whole of the North West Veluwe. The conclusion was drawn that it was not realistic to promote a process of community organization on a regional level only. There would have to be a complementary process of community organization on a more local basis. This would facilitate the process of distinguishing truly regional issues from the purely local ones, and provide a training ground for future regional leaders. . . .

The staff had asked permission of the Executive Committee to start a pilot project in promoting community organization on a local level. . . . A village and its immediate surroundings was selected for the project. It was generally known as a difficult village. "You can't achieve anything there" was a frequently heard opinion. Even the inhabitants of the village themselves would say: "We are a strange village, it is

almost impossible to start anything new here, we are very traditional."
The church is very important in the life of the villagers. Both
churches are extremely orthodox and people go to church very often.
Originally there had been one Protestant church, but sixty years ago
part of the council had walked out with about one third of the population following it. Seventy-five per cent of the population votes for an
extremely conservative party. Most people are very critical of the
government and, especially the farmers, may become quite violent
about governmental interference with farming. The village belongs to a
large municipality in which there is a strong competition between the
villages.

First, as much information as possible was collected from outside
resources so as not to disturb the village prematurely. The information
included two names of persons who according to an official of the
municipality had a sound view of the village problems. From this
information it could also be concluded which were the most important
groups into which the population was organized. The next step was a
series of talks with a number of leaders in the village. The aim would
be to get more information about the whole social situation and to find
out if it was desirable and possible to promote a process of community
organization. The introduction of the community organizer into the
village would be decisive for the way in which the rest of the project
would go. He was to introduce himself as somebody from the Foundation who would like to know whether he could be of any help to the
village. He would have to avoid being identified with a government
official and would have to maintain strict neutrality toward the
antagonisms between groups. His main task would be to improve
communications between the villagers and to promote objective discussions about the village problems.

The persons mentioned by the official turned out to be marginal men
and not leaders. Their information therefore had to be used with care.
From them the names of several leaders were obtained. Out of the
leaders in the village a choice was made on the basis of some assumptions derived from experience in other villages. Of course leaders of
both religious groups had to be included. Most of the old people could
be expected to be rather unresponsive to a proposal to re-examine
problems which they had learned to accept as unavoidable. Young

people would generally be more willing to embark upon an adventure but would not be respected by older people. Persons that did not belong to the indigenous population could be expected to have little authority. On the basis of these considerations persons were selected from both religious groups, of an age between 30 and 60 and belonging to the indigenous population. Every person visited was asked to mention the names of a few other leaders. From these names and from those already collected the next person to be interviewed was selected. After about 20 persons had been visited it looked as if a situation had been created which made a next move possible. The knowledge obtained fitted well into the general picture of the area. There was the usual tension between the religious groups. The church and the family were the most important channels for co-operation. The farmers and trade unions seemed to be unable to tackle the most important problems in their field. A music club, a glee club, and a sport club were functioning fairly well, but there was much opposition to them from one of the religious groups. The attitude of the population toward the municipal authorities was extremely critical. Municipal authorities were supposed to favor other villages with better roads and other public facilities. On the other hand, one would always hear the opinion that the less the village or its individual inhabitants were disturbed by interference from the side of the municipal, provincial, or national government the better it was. Communications between the villagers and the municipal authorities were quite insufficient.

Most persons interviewed mentioned several things they wanted improved in the village. Few of them however believed they would get any co-operation if they made an effort to do something about it. At the same time however several of the persons interviewed seemed to be a little fed up with the lack of co-operation between people from the two religious groups. It was obvious to the community organizer that there were untapped resources of co-operation. Somebody would have to create a situation in which these resources could become productive. Therefore the community organizer decided to ask all those he had visited if they would be willing to come to a meeting to discuss the possibilities of joined action. Everybody agreed to come although many were quite skeptical. The community organizer also spent some more time on discussions with two of the most promising leaders. His aim was to strengthen their capacity for leadership by sharing with them the insights into the situation which he had acquired himself.

At the meeting the community organizer first mentioned the fact that everybody had agreed to discuss possibilities of joined action. He also presented the list of things those present had wished to improve in the village. After this he suggested a discussion on the desirability of setting up some kind of village association. Several of those present expressed their doubts as to whether it would be possible to get the population out of its apathy. Few believed that the municipal government or the provincial authorities would be willing to help. Still it was decided to start the association and to elect a temporary committee. The community organizer then told those present that his task had ended but that he would be glad to help the committee as an adviser.

At the second public meeting, to which every villager had been invited, a committee of nine members was elected. Those present were asked to elect a committee which would represent both religious groups, the village as well as the surroundings, and also the different occupations. This was done. Only one "foreigner," a headmaster, was elected.

Several times the committee became involved in discussions in which tensions between groups in the village easily could have caused trouble. Every time the issues were frankly discussed, although at first some understandable embarrassment could be noticed. The diagnosis of the community organizer had been confirmed by the developments. In all nine members of the committee the conditions for effective co-operation had been potentially present. None of them as an individual, however, had been in a position to break the deadlock of group antagonism and other barriers to communication. Only somebody who was not personally involved in this situation had been able to break it. Therefore the most important task of the community organizer had been to keep open communications with everybody in the village. This was possible only after careful study of the situation with which he had been confronted.[2]

You will note that here the catalyst, unlike Miss Fairfax in Colton (Chapter IV), took care not to assume too much responsibility, but helped to build up the committee without taking too much on his own shoulders. In Chapter II we discussed how to recognize local leaders. Here we have some further evidence from the Netherlands. It is significant that the government official did not know who the real leaders were. However, after persistent interviewing, the community organizer seems to have learned who they were; and ultimately a committee of nine, presumably real leaders, were chosen by the village.

How may a committee be used to build unity and overcome destructive competition?

Bradford Military Hospital, U.S.A.

In 1946 there were over 500 employees at the Bradford Military Hospital, all dedicated in theory, at least, to one purpose: to serve the returned disabled ex-servicemen. Each medical department and each nonmedical unit, from the occupational therapy staff to the Red Cross office, showed loyalty to the ex-serviceman in a peculiar and destructive way. Each unit was competitively ambitious to outdo the other in serving the patient. Bitter rivalry ensued, resulting in serious schisms between departments. This lowered staff morale and was bad for the patients.

A new supervisor arrived and was put in charge of all nonmedical services. Sensing the disunity of the staff, she obtained permission from the superintendent to organize staff meetings on a new basis. Heretofore staff meetings had been few and from the top down. The staff had listened while a chief spoke.

The new supervisor stimulated lengthy discussion, in which nearly all the staff was prodded to take part. Common problems were raised which required joint action by several departments. Intense jealousies were aired, valuable time was consumed, and the entire staff combined in one thing: hating the new supervisor. Why could she not let them go about their work and let them hate the other departments without having to sit in the same room with them?

The new supervisor persisted. In staff meetings, problems involving several departments were delegated to joint committees for united study and report. Gradually mutual respect across departmental lines was built up and a more united point of view established. As bitter competition between departments subsided, attention was concentrated on united and improved service to the patient.[3]

Those who are critical of the slowness of the democratic process will argue that it need not be used within a governmental staff where it is possible to solve difficulties by the abrupt use of legal, autocratic authority. For example in the Indonesian case mentioned above, it would be unnecessary to take the time to convince the three Ministers of Health, Agriculture, and Education that they were engaged in a common battle against a joint foe and therefore should proceed in concert. Instead, it would be sufficient for the Prime Minister to call in each of them and say: "It's all very well for each of you to want to make a record for himself, but hereafter you must pool your plans and cease to act competitively. That's an order!"

I am convinced that even in government departments (although such an exercise of authority may be necessary at times) this makes for weaker administration than to take the time to build unity by more democratic methods; for real unity is a matter of the spirit and cannot be compelled.

Some years ago, before racial tension in our southern states was as openly discussed as it is today, a Negro student from Talladega College in Alabama came to take graduate courses at Columbia in social work. In a seminar on community organization a northern student suggested the advisability of organizing, in a southern city, an interracial committee to promote better relations between the races. The student from Talladega suggested that instead of meeting to discuss this issue directly, it would be better for an interracial committee to come together to work for some common purpose in which all were interested, such as public health. She said that as they came to know and respect each other as fellow workers for a common goal, instead of as representatives of different races, racial tension would be relaxed and they could proceed to work together in other matters. Rufus Jones, who was exceptionally adroit in uniting divergent groups among the Religious Society of Friends, once wrote:

Rufus Jones on Group Loyalty

If one does expect to change states of mind, habits of thought and attitudes of will, he will hardly begin by announcing that that is what he is doing! He will set about attaining some goal which will arouse group loyalty and create teamwork for the common end in view, and in the process new mental states get formed.[4]

How is a committee or a board meeting planned and conducted?

A standard work on the care of infants contains this caution: "Watch the baby's weight carefully, but not *too* carefully." Similar advice might be given those who are planning meetings, large and small. After community action has been initiated in a small way and begins to accelerate, the indirect leader will find himself continually planning meetings. Most of them will be committee meetings, but some may be intended to attract the whole community. We have all suffered through meetings that were poorly planned. That is the more usual fault.

Here is an example of a well-planned meeting held on Rarotonga which is one of the Cook Islands in the vicinity of New Zealand:

Rarotonga, New Zealand

In June, 1951, Mr. P. F. Henderson was appointed by the New Zealand government to the position of Acting Officer for Further

Education for the Cook Islands. He was formerly Acting Headmaster of the Avara School on Rarotonga. Being well acquainted with the islanders, it was hoped that he might initiate a successful "pilot project" involving adult education and the fostering of community spirit and the training of leaders who would eventually engage in community development work. A notice was sent to each village on Rarotonga calling a public meeting to elect village committees and to discuss the needs of each district. The first public meeting was held in the Ngatangiia district, which comprised three small villages and a larger village called Matavera.

A typical meeting was the first public meeting called at Ngatangiia on 21 June 1951 at 7 P.M. Approximately 100 residents of the district attended the meeting, men, women, youths, and girls being represented. Mr. Graham, the Education Officer, took the chair for the first part of the meeting and gave a general statement of the aims of the system, stressing the fact that the desire to take part in it must come from the people themselves. Mr. Henderson then gave a more detailed account of the actual activities that could be engaged in, for example, the showing of films and filmstrips, discussion groups, formal classes in advanced school subjects (mainly English), debating societies, health and welfare, arts and crafts, social activities, providing reading rooms, and so forth. Mr. Henderson and Mr. Graham then proposed that a committee be set up to run their own group. They also suggested that women as well as men might be represented on such a committee.

It was unanimously agreed by those present that women have equal representation with men. Further, the meeting voted unanimously that the election be by secret ballot, as suggested in the public notice calling the meeting. A committee of thirteen was decided upon, consisting of a president, a secretary, a treasurer, and ten delegates.

One man and one woman were to be chosen from each of the three small villages and two men and two women from the largest village (Matavera).

During the nominations for president the pastor nominated Pa Ariki, a chieftain who was not present. Immediately, the question arose as to whether nominations should be restricted to those present at the meeting, and it was decided by an almost unanimous vote that they should be so restricted. The pastor then said he considered that the committee should be composed of those holding high tribal rank, but it was insisted that they could not be elected unless they were present at the meeting.

Two nominations were then received for president. One was an elderly man of Mataiafo rank and of great influence in the community, and the other a young schoolteacher. As a result of the secret ballot, the younger man was elected.

On completion of the election of the committee, Mr. Graham and Mr. Henderson handed the meeting over to the new officers. The Matavera village spokesman offered the free use of a building in his district. It was not expected that the government would pay for equipment and so forth. Those present felt that they themselves must raise the money to be self-supporting.

The following topics were listed as those most desired at the beginning of the adult education program:

1. English lessons for the older people with little understanding of that language.
2. Advanced classes for those younger people who had recently left school.
3. Health and welfare talks and discussions.
4. Increased use of films (especially of other peoples, and of industries).
5. Social activities.

Mr Henderson suggested that the Adult Education Office print in English and Maori a weekly review of world news and distribute it to all groups at the center. This proposal met with instant approval.[5]

If any difficulties were encountered thereafter, they were not recorded. By February, 1952, Ngatangiia had its own community center controlled entirely by the local people with subcommittees operating the various activities including a library; a clubroom; an arts, crafts, and sewing room; a film projection and indoor sports room; a medical clinic; a carpenter workshop; and a kitchen. Two acres of land had been set aside by the members of the center as an experimental farm, with the help and guidance of the director of agriculture. This successful outcome would seem to have resulted from careful planning of the initial meeting.

However, meetings can be planned too carefully. When I first served as executive of a local social agency, I was overanxious that meetings should proceed with smoothness and dispatch. I therefore prepared the agenda with great care. The items for discussion were numbered, and where a formal motion was appropriate I added in parentheses "Motion by Mr. So-and-So." I interviewed Mr. So-and-So in advance, asked him to make the motion, and gave him a typewritten copy of the proposed motion.

The agenda was then mimeographed and distributed to all committee members as they entered the room. All went well for the first three items. The chairman, who was equally desirous of conducting the meeting with dispatch, called off each item in the order listed. After brief discussion, the Mr. So-and-So whose name was listed after that item drew a typewritten motion from his pocket, read it, and moved its adoption. There were no negative votes and we moved on to the fourth item, after which appeared the words "Motion by Mr. Winfield." The chairman asked the executive to explain this item. There were one or two questions and then the chair asked: "Well, gentlemen, what is your plea- sure?" Nobody said anything, but all looked at Mr. Winfield. His face became red as he searched frantically through his pockets and then blurted out: "King, where is that damn motion?" Everybody roared, the executive's copy of the proposed motion was handed to Mr. Winfield, he read it, and it was unanimously adopted amid much laughter.

This may seem humorous, but such planning violates the most important purpose of a citizens' committee, which is to encourage members to participate and make the movement *theirs* so that they can carry on when the indirect leader is gone. If you are serving as such a leader, keep in mind that the real test of the quality of your leadership will be *what happens after you have left the community.*

Hertfield Community Chest, U.S.A.

A friend of mine whom I shall call Bob had been executive of the Hertfield Community Chest for twenty years. He had made a national reputation for conducting successful campaigns. At last he resigned to accept a more responsible national position. In all those twenty years his board had never failed to adopt anything that he proposed. I asked him how he had managed never to. be voted down. "Well," said the practical Bob, "I made up the agenda, and I shopped around a little first. There are always three or four who make up the mind of the board. If I didn't have the votes I didn't put the matter on the agenda." "But," I suggested, "wouldn't it be a good plan to let them vote you down occasionally, just for a change?" "Say," replied Bob, "suppose they got the habit; where would you be then?" I asked another social worker who had worked in Hertfield what kind of board Bob had. "The attendance was terrible," was the reply; "three or four people made all the decisions in advance. The rest of them weren't so dumb. What was the use of their coming if it was all cut and dried anyway? So they stayed away."

From Bob's practical standpoint his technique was uniformly successful. From the standpoint of the welfare of the community, he was a failure. He left behind him a committee unable to carry on without him or even to select a good successor. Citizen participation in community action should be an adult education experience of the highest order. This cannot happen if the committee is manipulated into always blindly approving the proposals of an overdominant executive. Again and again in our practice we may feel that we must use short-cut methods to get immediate results. We may be right, but let us make the choice with our eyes open, knowing that winning our immediate objective may mean losing our ultimate goal, which should be to leave the community better than we found it and to give such leadership that our local colleagues may be better able to carry on because we have enabled them to have a creative experience.

Who should be included on the committee?

Sooner or later in most community action the time will come when a committee is to be appointed to conduct some part of the work. You may have an opportunity to suggest who should be chosen. If there is a real difference of opinion among the citizens of the community about what the committee shall do, do not yield to the temptation of suggesting only persons who agree with you. It may prove better to have the opposition represented. Here is a case in point.

Beechmont Mental Health Society, U.S.A.

For years the Community Council in Beechmont had worked to awaken citizens to the need for a mental health clinic similar to the one Miss Parker had succeeded in getting started in Woodhurst. The greatest obstacle was the Medical Association led by Dr. Block. He was head of the Beechmont Hospital and of the YMCA. For years no movement had been a success in Beechmont unless Dr. Block was connected with it. He was of the old school of medicine and declared that the new science of psychiatry was "hooey."

The younger members of the Medical Association feared Dr. Block and would not oppose him. The council invited Dr. C.E.A. Winslow of the Yale School of Public Health to come to Beechmont and speak in favor of a mental clinic. Dr. Block was invited by mail, and I was requested to call on him personally and urge him to come even if he disagreed with Dr. Winslow. He came late and sat in the back of the room and made uncomplimentary remarks under his breath during the address and finally stepped out early as though not wishing to be associated with the affair.

Six months later, when I had left Beechmont, I received a letter on the letterhead of the new Beechmont Mental Health Society. To my astonishment there was Dr. Block's name as a member of the board of directors. I telephoned to a friend in Beechmont and asked the explanation of the miracle. "Oh, it was not so difficult," my friend said. "When it became clear that the new society was going to be formed, I went to Dr. Block and asked him if he didn't think some sane, sensible conservative should be on the new board to help them 'keep their feet on the ground.' He agreed that they certainly needed a 'balance wheel.' I proposed that he serve in that capacity and he fell for it."

Probably Dr. Block was influenced not only by flattery but by a fear that the movement might succeed without him, in which case he would lose the reputation of always being in on everything which succeeded in Beechmont. Be that as it may, the other doctors, when they saw Dr. Block's name on the board, decided that it would be safe to co-operate with the new clinic, which prospered accordingly.

Monroe Budget Committee, U.S.A.

In the city of Monroe I had a somewhat similar experience when I was serving as executive of the Monroe United Community Fund. We were seriously impeded in establishing the Fund by the opposition of Banker X and a substantial group of citizens influenced by his opinion. At last to my horror, the Nominating Committee proposed to add Banker X to the Budget Committee the next year. I opposed this nomination. Mr. X was a very negative person. As a banker he had said "no" so habitually that his face was set that way. He was not social-minded, I complained, and would merely seek to keep down all appropriations to our member agencies. I was overruled, and Mr. X was elected. It was just as I feared except that he proved less astute than I expected. He asked detailed questions about such minor items as postage and transportation, which he understood, but major items such as relief and family budgets got by him without comment because he did not know what questions to ask. On transportation he actually made an affirmative contribution, suggesting a plan for joint purchase of gasoline and other automobile supplies at reduced prices. But in general he sought to get a low settlement from the spokesman for a social agency by wearing him out with voluminous questions.

In executive sessions at the close of the budget hearings, the rest of the committee had a hard time with him. Fortunately most of them were experienced and social-minded. He said that because times were hard and contributors could not afford to give as much as last year, the total asked of the public must be *less* than last year. The rest of us contended that just because times were hard the need was greater and we must ask *more*. Slowly we wore him out. Legitimate requests for funds from all the agencies amounted to double the total raised the year before. Other members of the committee were more intelligent than he was in finding items that might be postponed until another year with little detriment to the community. At last we reached a unanimous judgment on asking 40 per cent more than the preceding year, and even Banker X signed the report.

Thereafter he was the greatest asset we had. When the report was published in the papers it shocked the town and particularly the conservative group which followed his lead, but seeing his name annexed to the recommendations, they said: "Well, if Banker X agrees, there can't be any water in it." We made our goal.

This technique of drawing a representative of the opposition into the planning group was used by President Roosevelt when he sent Senator Vandenburg, a conservative Republican, to represent the United States at San Francisco where the United Nations was born. President Wilson failed to use this technique in a similar crisis after World War I. Who knows but that its use might have forestalled the bitter attacks by Senator Lodge (grandfather of the present Henry Cabot Lodge) and got us into the League of Nations? Might greater skill in community action have saved the League and prevented World War II?

Generally we fear to put our opponent on the committee lest he defeat us there. But if he represents a strong group with whom we must come to grips sooner or later, we have little to lose and much to gain by this technique. We might better fight him at close range than delay the action and have him defeat us in the community at large. By courting the conflict early we at least learn the attitude of the opposition more accurately so that we can prepare to meet it. At best, we may conciliate the opposition by including them in the planning group from the start. Furthermore, we may find that their views modify ours and that the resulting plan is better than either.

How can committees be used in a community self-study?

In Woodhurst (Chapter IV) Miss Parker encouraged the Community Council to appoint a study committee of nine citizens to examine into the need for a mental health clinic. This is called a Community Self-Study. The state society for mental health loaned them a trained worker to serve as secretary of the committee. She examined the case loads of each of the welfare agencies and brought the information to the committee. But *they* made the decisions, approved the language of the report and the recommendations, and affixed their signatures. The enterprise was not only fact finding but interpretation. *They,* the committee of citizens (a chemical engineer, three housewives, an employment manager, and so on) became convinced of the facts and the recommendations became *theirs.* Then they set out to convince the town, and their efforts were successful.

The operation of a Community Self-Study is not so easy as this sounds, but there is far more probability that it will result in constructive action than if the study is the exclusive work of an outside expert. The chief thing to remember is that a Community Self-Study has a twofold purpose: to find the facts and at the same time to interpret them to the community so that it will be inspired to take needed action. A survey by a sincere social scientist is vastly different. He must remain unbiased in finding the facts. How to get his report accepted by the public is not his concern. Nor can he have amateur citizens taking part with him lest that might affect the scientific accuracy of his work. He must work quietly. The Community Self-Study must be conducted noisily; that is, the public must be associated with it from the start, and all the arts of publicity should be practiced to awaken the community to an interest in the subject being studied. We must remind ourselves again that we can proceed no faster than the understanding and consent of the majority of the citizens, and that what they are not up on, they are likely to be down on.

The expert Social Survey proceeds modestly and quietly until the findings and recommendations are written. Then (perhaps after the expert has gone) comes the difficulty of explaining the whole thing to the public. But this is too late. The best interpretation is *participation;* hence the need for a committee of lay citizens to take an active part in the work from the start. From the standpoint of publicity, half the news value is gone when the report is completed. The newspapers should be intimately related to the study as it goes along. This may have some surprising complications, as for example:

Medford Community Self-Study, U.S.A.

As the city of Medford grew in size an increasing number of Negroes came to live in this New England city. No Negro girls came to the YWCA. The board of directors debated whether they should establish a "Phyllis Wheatley Branch" for Negro girls with a Negro staff as had been done in a neighboring city. The YWCA executive was doubtful whether such segregation was desirable, but many on her board favored it. This might have developed into an emotional impulse to meet the need quickly, and a campaign to establish a separate branch might have been launched forthwith.

To avoid this, the YWCA executive wisely suggested a Community Self-Study to be sponsored by the Community Council in which all social and health services for colored citizens should be examined and recommendations for improved services made.

This plan was approved by the YWCA board and by the Community Council (of which I was then the executive). A bi-racial committee of twenty-four citizens was chosen to conduct what was called the "Colored Problems Study." As secretary of the study committee we were fortunate in securing Miss Radborne, a Negro student from the New York School of Social Work. The school was glad to assign her to work in Medford as part of her field work training. Miss Radborne was to arrive in town on the first Monday in January to start work. Miss Ibsen, my associate at the Community Council, was an expert in publicity. We determined to seek newspaper publicity from the beginning. Miss Ibsen obtained a photograph of Miss Radborne and made a two-column cut for the newspaper. This required a two-column story which Miss Ibsen released a few days before Miss Radborne's arrival.

Early Monday morning the city editor called me on the phone and asked if Miss Radborne was there. I said that her train would arrive in a few minutes. "Send her right down to my office," said he and hung up the phone. When Miss Radborne came in, she, Miss Ibsen, and I went into a huddle. What could be the meaning of the city editor's request? Should we let her go down to see him before she had started work? We had determined to court newspaper publicity, but this seemed going it rather strong. However, Miss Radborne was a courageous person, and we let her go. The sequel proved an anti-climax. The editor's daughter was to be in a high school debate on the Fourteenth Amendment (providing equal rights for Negroes). Would Miss Radborne help her? (Miss Radborne did, and the editor's daughter won.) Perhaps this had something to do with the remarkable amount of newspaper space devoted to the Colored Problems Study throughout its progress.

If you are attempting to guide a Community Self-Study of any magnitude, you will find it useful to copy our technique in regard to several working subcommittees. We had six: Employment, Recreation, Housing, Health, Family Welfare, and Child Welfare. The purpose of these subcommittees was twofold. What might be called the ulterior purpose was to involve more people in the study. Each working group had five or six members, all *additional* to the Central Committee except the chairman who sat on the Central Committee. Thus we got some thirty more citizens to participate in the enterprise, thereby arousing their interest.

The main reason for these working committees was to secure persons who could give more time to fact finding than could members of the Central Committee. We tried to get on each functional subcommittee professional persons related to that function: doctors and nurses on the Health Committee, family case workers on the Family Welfare Committee; et cetera. These professionals were charged with the task of securing from state and national experts in their fields advice as to recommendations for action based on the facts discovered. It may be asked: if six subcommittees were useful, why not eight or ten, thereby involving more people? Here we are limited by the difficulty of securing a secretary for each working committee. No such group can secure the best results without one among their number who can give a very substantial block of time each day to the work—more than the others can give. We were able to secure three social workers for this purpose, their organizations releasing them for half time. Miss Ibsen served as secretary of the Health Committee. These six secretaries were charged with the actual drafting of the subcommittees' reports. After approval by each subcommittee they were forwarded to the Central Committee for possible revision and action.

Each day during the study some news story was issued to the local paper: announcement of members who had accepted committee appointments, statements of when various committees were to meet, when a report was to be considered by the Central Committee; and so on. One of the first things the Central Committee did was to ask the heads of all the social agencies to come together with the Committee and state orally just what services they performed for colored citizens. It was rather a meager showing except for the statement of the Chairman of the Recreation Commission. [This city department served many boys and girls of both races.] The president of the Boy Scouts boasted that they had two Negro troops, one in each of the two Negro churches. The YMCA president said that three or four Negro boys used their gymnasium. The president of the Girl Scouts was the last to report, and she was embarrassed. The "best" girls belonged to the Scouts. Indeed it was a rather fashionable organization. Until that meeting there had been no plan for Negro Girl Scouts. The president arose and unblushingly reported that they were planning to organize a Negro troop. She left the hall hurriedly and started right in to organize one.[6]

Here is an essential difference between an expert Social Survey and a Community Self-Study. If, during the latter, the study begins

to indicate a desirable course of action which can be readily undertaken, it will probably be taken at once and have already been
accomplished before it can be listed in an orderly list of Recommendations in the final report. During a very ambitious Community Self-Study in the city of Washington it began to appear that
a new Department of Correction would probably be recommended,
separate from the Public Welfare Department. Two members of
Congress who were serving on the committee each hastened to
draft a bill to that effect to get the credit for its introduction in
Congress.

*   *   *

Summary.   Most community action begins with the formation
of a committee. Membership on the committee should therefore be
carefully planned with a view to what it is hoped the committee
may accomplish. One of the most important purposes of a committee is to bring about unity in the community. Committee meetings should be carefully planned, but not so rigidly as to prevent
freedom of discussion. It is well to include on the committee
persons of different points of view if they represent substantial
segments of the population. In a Community Self-Study a representative central committee and functional subcommittees can be
used to secure participation by many members of the community.

VII. COMMUNITY AND NEIGHBORHOOD COUNCILS

When is a community council needed?

In farming districts in the United States, there is a marvelous machine called a *separator*. In my boyhood it ran by boy power; now it runs by electricity. The crank is turned, the milk is poured into the hopper, and then, by some miraculous combination of forces known as specific gravity and centrifugal force (I am not an expert in physics, so do not take my explanation of this phenomenon too seriously!), the cream is driven out of one spout and the skim milk out of another. In our community life most of the forces which affect us are separators, and there is a superabundance of centrifugal force. We separate for our recreation, our religion, our politics. We separate into our luncheon clubs, our women's clubs, our lodges, and our other fraternal bodies. We unite, yes, but in small bundles and in a manner which makes us competitive with other groups that have to appeal to the same public for sponsorship and support. In this there is some healthy rivalry, but it can become destructive when we view our community as a whole. There is a desperate need in all communities for what might be called a new machine to generate *centripetal force*—an integrator.

You for whom this book is intended, wherever you may be, have the opportunity to build this needed mechanism. People are united by common interests, by a common enthusiasm. You have the opportunity and duty to help initiate and generate this unifying force. A student of mine once coined the phrase: "A community is first a spirit and then an area." Merely living together in the same spot does not make us a real community. Only when we are united in spirit do we become that.

In our first chapter we lauded the freedom of any citizen in any American community to start a new movement "without reference to any bureaucrat," as de Tocqueville put it. This is a fine thing—this drawing people together into relatively small bundles for community action to meet a *particular* need. The use of what we called the "snowball" method produces a small cohesive group of people with a common interest. The more intense their enthusiasm for meeting the particular need, the more danger there is that they may become destructively competitive with other energized groups working to meet other particular needs.

When attempting to bring into being a new united community fund in an industrial city in the United States, I have sometimes been tempted to regard agency enthusiasm only as a destructive thing. If no citizen cared any more for the Boy Scouts or the Red Cross than for the YMCA or the Children's Aid Society how easy it would be to push them all around to form the perfect integrator! But of course without these narrower loyalties there would be nothing to co-ordinate. If nobody cared, there would be no social work.

There are times when national patriotism seems a bloody and destructive force, but of course what our world needs is not fewer loyalties, but a larger and all-embracing loyalty to keep our little loyalties in balance.

If you are a village level worker in one of the so-called under-developed countries, you may see nothing in common between your job and that of the Secretary-General of the United Nations, but you are both building unity. A united village or a united world is a far better place for children to be born into. A nation or the world is no stronger than the people in it. So who shall say that those of you who build at the village level have not as important a task as those who guide international policy?

One thing is clear. No project on which you may be at work is in itself as important as its ultimate effect on the community, the unity that comes from a common enthusiasm and joint accomplishment giving the people self-confidence to go forward to further and greater accomplishments.

A timid man once visited a mental institution. He was shown around by a small, frail-looking psychiatrist. As they went from room to room the inmates seemed to become larger and more formidable, with bulging muscles and glaring eyes. At last the visitor could stand it no longer. He grasped his guide by the arm and pulled him out into the corridor. "Doctor," he whispered, "do you realize what would happen to you if these men should get together?" The little psychiatrist replied without the slightest trepidation, "If these men could get together, they wouldn't be where they are now."

If our fellow citizens in your community or mine could get together, they wouldn't be where *they* are now. In other words, the many things which, in every community, need to be done for a better life would already be under way. Let us emphasize again that we have experts among us who *know* enough to revolutionize community life for the better. All that is lacking is group unity to make community action possible. Unless we are willing to barter our freedom for autocracy, progress must wait until we can arouse group loyalty and create teamwork for the common good.

Fortunately the best way to create such teamwork is to awaken enthusiasm in divergent groups for some common purpose in which they share a joint interest. The unity thus engendered concerning one joint enterprise then makes it possible to get together for other goals which need to be jointly undertaken. The best community integrator yet devised seems to be a community council. Such a council is more than just another committee. It generally consists of delegates from each organized group in town, who meet together to share their ideas and plans for improving the community, somewhat as the delegates from various nations meet together in the Assembly of the United Nations.

In the United States the council movement began in a few cities shortly before World War I, and gathered momentum thereafter. At first it was confined to agencies concerned with social welfare and public health, with privately supported agencies taking the lead. Government agencies concerned with recreation, education, and health were drawn in. This was important because without such an integrator there was danger that a schism might develop between public and private agencies. It was found that the best role for a private agency was to start a new movement (like that of mental health in Woodhurst: see Chapter IV), and then when it had been accepted by a majority of the population, transfer the enterprise to be operated and supported by the government.

One of the advantages of a community council is to serve as a forum where governmental and nongovernmental organizations can work together and plan together. There is some danger that a private agency may seek to perpetuate itself after a function which it has thoroughly demonstrated has been so well accepted that it can be financed by taxation and administered officially, leaving private efforts free to pioneer in other needed fields. When the movement has become governmental, the council can still be useful in maintaining citizen interest in it. Otherwise public interest may lapse and the movement suffer. In the plan for free dental care for school children in Monroe, mentioned in Chapter IV, the movement might have died if there had not been a strong community council to fight for its continuance.

How should a community council be organized?

Community councils, as discussed in this chapter, are not to be confused with village councils, or city councils, which are elected governmental bodies. The councils we are considering have no governmental authority. They are purely advisory. I have heard a member describe the council as "an organization in which to convince each other." A community council, however, if it proceeds wisely, may have great influence. In the early days of the council movement in the United States only social agencies were admitted to membership. (We are not discussing here community welfare councils as found in most large cities in the United States.) The recent tendency is toward a more inclusive council of all organizations working for civic betterment, including men's service clubs, town planning organizations, and so on. Most councils are composed mainly of delegates appointed by these organizations themselves, with provision for a minority of individual members-at-large invited by the council.

This form of organization has two strong advantages but one real drawback. By bringing representatives of all organized groups together, this makes for unity and strength and the elimination of destructive competition among the member organizations. It also makes for joint planning instead of competitive planning. It tends to focus everyone's attention on the needs of the whole community, rather than upon increasing the prestige of one member organization in the competition for public support.

All this is to the good, and in a town of not more than five thousand inhabitants like Colton, where Miss Fairfax promoted a council (see Chapter IV), this form of organization would be quite adequate. In Colton the population was fairly homogeneous and any interested citizen, irrespective of his wealth or social position, might well be active in one of the member organizations and have some voice in the deliberations of the community council; not so in New York City or Delhi, India, Newark, New Jersey or Johannesburg, South Africa. In such great centers with great extremes of wealth and poverty, the tendency is for a council of agency delegates to become less democratic. They may be motivated by the best motives, and plan and work wisely for the less advantaged portions of the population, but these latter are not likely to be represented in the planning. The council will be *for* and not *with* those to be helped. The situation will be more like that in Bang Pa Kong (Chapter V), where all agencies were represented in the planning except the farmers for whom the whole enterprise was intended.

To meet this difficulty it becomes necessary to stimulate the organization (at least in large cities) of neighborhood councils and even of block or local zone organizations, to include those citizens who should be most intimately concerned with community development.

How should a neighborhood council be organized?

Professor Morris L. Eisenstein, formerly of the Graduate School of Social Work at Ohio State University, has served as a catalyst in organizing neighborhood councils in Brooklyn and in East Harlem, New York City. He has thus described the basic philosophy underlying the form of organization:

Neighborhood Organization in East Harlem, U.S.A.

The experiment in neighborhood organization in East Harlem differs from others in that it attempted to approach this working-class, deteriorated, and blighted area from the point of view of the people living in it, with an awareness that their culture, values, and goals were in most respects different from the middle-class goals and aims of the agency responsible for the program.

Neighborhood organization is a process of organizing people, where they live, to create conditions favorable for bringing about social change which broadens the base of democracy and diffuses power through an ever-wider circle of the population. To be effective it needs to develop roots in the community, to become part of the community.

It is imperative, then, that the aims and strivings of the people in the neighborhood should become the basis of any program if it is to succeed. It is not sufficient for these goals to be reflected in the program; the people must participate in the formation of the objectives, aims, and program. This does not mean that an agency consisting of outsiders cannot, therefore, institute or stimulate a program of action in a community. It does mean that in the initiation of an activity or program the people of the community must be brought in at all levels in helping to set up the program.

The agency has the further responsibility of consciously maintaining an awareness that it must continually hand over more and more control to the neighborhood people as well as seek out avenues and means of enlarging the base of participation among the people with whom it is working.

Such an approach requires some change in our orientation toward working with people. It demands getting out from behind the protection of buildings and desks, where we meet the people on our terms, and going out where the people are—their homes and organizations, the street and wherever the people congregate—and meeting them on their terms. This means coming to a community without any predetermined judgment of their culture and values, but rather with the desire to learn about, understand, and accept their way of life and the basis for their judgments and behavior. Learning their language and habits becomes part of the job. It means working with people on a basis of equality with no attempts to impose values and ideas upon them. It means subordinating yourself and your agency to the decisions of the people of the neighborhood. Being tested by the people continually (because they distrust you and your motives) becomes a part of your daily life and you must learn to accept it as part of your relationship with the people. You must be prepared (as a student, in one of the agencies doing block organization, recorded after his first day in the neighborhood), to feel naked and unprotected.

An important consideration in neighborhood organization is that it is inclusive. In organizing, all people are acceptable regardless of any other consideration but that they are interested in helping to do something about changing conditions in the community for the better. This approach is not to be qualified in any other way. Regardless of religion, race, politics, age, sex, method of earning a living or any other criterion—all people are acceptable—the poolroom owner, barkeeper, church member, pimp, gambler, doctor, lawyer—so long as they are desirous of helping accomplish the goals set by the members of the neighborhood organization. This is crucial to the success of working with the community—if we are to unify its people around common issues.

This does not imply that all people will join—many may see a threat to their position and power if neighborhood organization gets effectively under way. But it is important to establish at least one place where people of different persuasion and point of view can come together to explore areas of common interest in spite of their differences, which in some cases may even be fundamental in nature. To exclude any group which is ready to work for the benefit of the neighborhood from participation, sets up the conditions for excluding other groups, and starts off by emphasizing divisions in the community as well as establishing a certain exclusiveness in the organization. The greatest loss is that the community is denied the benefits of the experience and the possible contributions of the members of the excluded group.

Some of the people working in the field of intergroup relations recognize that the use of force and the intensification of conflict have brought about desirable results in some instances. But many reject the use of conflict and force as a means of solving intergroup conflicts. Neighborhood organization recognizes the existence of conflict in society and accepts the use of force when necessary as one of the possible methods for resolving conflict, and does not hesitate to use it when other methods have failed.

Traditionally neighborhood organization has consisted of federating in some form the already existing organizations in a community— usually in the form of a neighborhood council. The structure may have varied, but essentially the form was that of representatives of organized groups meeting together. This, of course, completely left out those people, of whom there are great numbers, who belonged to no organization. Block organization on the other hand attempts to organize people on the basis of where they live, regardless of whether they belong to an organization or not.[1]

You will notice that representation on the neighborhood council, under this plan, is not by delegates who are from organizations which work in the area and who are controlled by persons living outside the neighborhood. The council is composed of local representatives chosen by each block. A block in this case includes all people living on either side of a given street between one cross street and the next. While Morris Eisenstein was pioneering in block and neighborhood organization in Brooklyn and East Harlem, a similar experiment was being carried on in Delhi, India by B. Chatterjee, Director of Urban Community Development of Delhi, and Marshall B. Clinard, Consultant on Urban Community Development, of the Ford Foundation. They have described the plan as follows:

Neighborhood Organization in Delhi, India

"Vikas Mandals," or Citizens' Development Councils, are small groups of people living in a local area (about 250 to 400 families or 1250 to 2000 persons) who are organized through the stimulation of urban community organizers. They serve as planning-and-action agencies in order to tackle problems and needs of the area. They operate through democratically elected executive committees consisting of representatives from smaller areas (15 to 20 families) known as zones. After the council is elected, a general meeting is called to adopt a constitution and to elect office bearers including a president, vice-president, secretary, and treasurer. The council in turn selects sub-committees to work on problems in the area. The Vikas Mandal then determines the area problems and formulates action programs.

A male and a female organizer are assigned to form each Vikas Mandal. These will be part of a large team who, working together under a neighborhood organizer, will be forming a neighborhood council which is made up of several Vikas Mandals.

. . . . .

Since India is a developing country, profound changes must be made in the standard of living and economic opportunities, and this is certainly a reasonable long-term approach, along with plans for slum clearance and better housing, for millions of city dwellers. This goal cannot be fully accomplished in the near future. Meanwhile, cities will continue to grow by leaps and bounds. What must be done, therefore, is to make changes in the lives of the people within the present framework, and with the resources now available. These changes can be of a limited physical nature, such as improved drains, water facilities and latrines, organized recreation, accompanied by changes in social conditions and general outlook. After all, it is the "slum mentality" rather than the physical slum which is of basic importance, and this cannot be explained entirely on the basis of poverty.

It is possible to tackle successfully difficult urban conditions, as has been demonstrated in Delhi, through a scheme of urban community development, since the community betterment is brought about through people's support and initiative and their mobilization on a systematic basis. Urban community development must be realistic in view of the enormity of the problems, the extreme density and rapid growth of the population, and the limited resources available.

Urban community development is based on these assumptions:

1. Change can best be brought about by working with groups of people rather than working with individuals, since slum life is largely a product of group practices and customs.
2. People in an urban community need assistance in recognizing their needs and in organizing themselves to achieve the desired objectives.
3. People living in squalid living conditions do not generally accept the conditions as natural and inevitable.
4. The program of urban development is limited only to those areas and problems where there is possibility of self-help.
5. And programs such as major housing and unemployment are generally outside the scope of the urban development program

as they call for action at the state and national levels. However, urban people, when organized, can help and supplement governmental efforts even in these areas. . . .

The pilot scheme of urban community development was instituted in Delhi in September, 1958, with a view to find out the possibilities of bringing, in local areas, improvements based on self-help principles and devising suitable organizational patterns and effective techniques. The program was made possible by a grant from Ford Foundation to the Delhi Municipal Corporation through the Health Ministry. The Municipal Corporation of Delhi also contributes an increasing contribution of the cost annually.

. . . . .

Selected slum areas in the city were surveyed and suitable areas selected for initiating the experimental projects. . . . The six areas selected, as under, have distinctive population, caste, and occupational composition, physical condition, and so on, factors which might help or hinder community organization:

1. A colony built for the rehabilitation of squatters from shack bustees.
2. Slum area in a highly congested low-income part of the city with relative unity in occupation and religious background. (Muslims)
3. Slum area in a highly congested part of the city in a lower-income bracket but with relative unity in occupational and religious background.
4. An area predominantly of industrial workers.
5. Congested area with considerable diversity in occupation, economic class, and caste.
6. A refugee colony with cultural and recreational problems.[2]

How can a neighborhood council help in urban community development?

Daniel and Hope Murrow were in charge of "Project House" in East Harlem, which is operated according to the philosophy stated by Morris Eisenstein above:

East Harlem Youth Council and Block Council, U.S.A.

My husband and I, both social workers, together direct the East Harlem Projects House of the American Friends Service Committee. We live with our baby daughter in this four-storey, renovated, brownstone house in Puerto Rican East Harlem. Part of our job is to supervise a group of eight volunteers who live in their own rooms or apartments here on East 111 Street, in order to come to understand slum problems first hand, and to seek ways of stimulating natural leadership and initiative in a depressed area. All members of the group, ranging in age from 21 to 35, work outside of our program to support themselves, mainly in the area of education or social service, and volunteer in their hours after work to help on neighborhood programs. This has been, to date, a self-supporting project with members contributing to a pool to cover expenses. The philosophy behind this project is that any activity taken on should be self-supporting, as we are not in East Harlem to give funds or to take over a leadership role, but to have a catalytic role. We also help to direct other special activities of the Service Committee which take place in the Projects House. These are: weekend seminar-workcamps to which come high school and college students who want to learn more of slum problems and to help neighbors to paint and plaster their apartments; weekend Institutional Units, during which college-age young people interested in the problems of mental illness volunteer in the wards of the local mental hospital and study aspects of mental health; and seminars of various kinds, generally focusing on the study of urban problems, for young people interested in social service or social science.

The American Friends Service Committee is a pacifist organization, an outgrowth of the Quaker religion, whose main purpose is to stimulate people in troubled areas to help themselves and others, and to encourage peaceful, friendly relationships among different groups, wherever there is conflict.

Since we live on our job, our schedules are flexible, and we are available most of our waking hours. For me, important contacts are made while marketing or walking with our 16-month-old baby. Many hours of each day are spent in spontaneous conversation with neighbors of all ages, from which spring our most creative projects.

Community people are involved, as leaders and members, in all our social action projects. We wouldn't consider one without them, as stimulating their leadership is our major purpose for being here. Let me describe some of our current and recent programs, relating to community improvement; in most cases, the community is limited to our area of East Harlem:

A. *East Harlem Youth Council*

Since July of 1959, there has been a Council meeting in our projects house, under our guidance, made up of all the major youth clubs or teen-age gangs in East Harlem. At first their focus was on preventing inter-gang conflicts, and they held regular organizational meetings, as well as special mediation meetings. Now that gang violence has become less of a problem in the area, they are most concerned with finding creative outlets for young people—dramatics, work projects, trips to other communities. The Council has its own leaders, notably the young 24-year-old ex-gang-leader who first set the Council in motion, and is its chairman. They formulate all their own plans, but we see them daily for informal talks, generally in the evening, to share ideas and support the most positive aspects of their plans.

B. *East 111 Street Neighborhood Council*

This organization, stimulated by us, but with its own leaders, is constantly changing in membership and purpose. It evolved out of sidewalk discussions of poor sanitary conditions on the street, which brought forth the suggestion that neighbors should found a Council with representatives from each building to work on improving these conditions. The Council's first big event was the "Big Sweep," a block party with the theme of sanitation, in which neighbors swept the block clean before festivities as a symbolic gesture of the way they would like to keep it. Neighbors, young and old, were involved in all aspects of planning—making posters, getting permits, although we were always working along with them. Later, members of the block council collected money for Christmas decorations by going from door to door, together with our volunteers; they helped to plan and put up the decorations, and were very proud that our block was the only one in the area so decorated. More recently, Council members have been especially concerned about the problem of drug addiction in our area. They sent two representatives to an East Harlem Town Meeting with the Mayor and asked well-thought-out questions of him. Our Projects House was used as a polling place [at elections], and one Council member volunteered his time to help neighbors learn enough to pass the literacy test.

C. *Special Youth Activities*

One of the main purposes of our Projects House is to serve as a bridge between people of different social, racial, economic, and educational backgrounds—particularly young people. When seminars and workcamps, involving middle-class young people, use the house, they are enthusiastically participated in by local youngsters. Lasting friendships between the two groups, with visits back and forth, are formed this way. This is a subtle, but basic, type of social action, for these youngsters of disparate backgrounds have the opportunity to understand each other, and form the basis for working together in the future. In this case we, as staff, merely set up situations in which the young people can interact, and their own desire to know each other does the rest.

The main problem was not so much to train and develop neighborhood leaders, but to discover, recognize, and work with those who already existed. Often these leaders were operating in subtle but powerful ways within their own subgroups, but had never been recognized by an agency—for instance, some of the young gang leaders, when supported in the right direction, proved to have tremendous influence for good, both in and out of their own groups.

One of our most important functions is to try to help these natural leaders to resolve the many personal problems which invariably beset them in this complex, deteriorated neighborhood where such problems as drug addiction are common. We find that it involves a multidisciplined approach of casework, group work and community organization to be able to relate to the individual and his problems, and still be able to see his creative function within his group and neighborhood, detracting from neither.[3]

The "Committee for the Welfare of Yambele" in Puerto Rico (see Chapter IV) was, in effect, a neighborhood council organized along the lines recommended by Morris Eisenstein. It succeeded in converting a suburban slum composed of squatters into a legal and healthful community, and securing for it the needed public utilities. Here is a similar experience from Newark, New Jersey:

Clinton Hill, Newark, U.S.A.

Clinton Hill is a fringe area bordering on Newark's old Third Ward, formerly the Jewish and then the Negro ghetto, and now the locale for extensive mass clearance projects. The report of the Mayor's Commission on Group Relations for 1959 stated: "Though Negroes are moving out in all directions, the tendency is to move toward the south, to Clinton Hill, more than anywhere else." The area numbers 40,000 lower middle- and working-class residents on 100 city blocks. Many residents possess solid traditions of organizational work in church, fraternal, and civil rights groups; they form the backbone of the council.

The manner in which the Clinton Hill council got started influenced its structure and policy. In 1955 about two dozen residents and community leaders, concerned over panic selling, zoning violations, and declining city services, and eager to welcome new residents, began the group. After a series of house meetings, the Council caught on at an open community conference called to draw up a program. Code enforcement, better schools, and improved city services were the key demands. Memberships at one dollar a year poured in. First it built mass membership among tenants and homeowners. Most members formed themselves into block-branches consisting of the residents in houses which faced each other on a street. Each block-branch handled immediate questions (nuisances, dwelling maintenance, social affairs) and elected leaders to represent it on higher council bodies. Then an advisory board was formed of top neighborhood leaders, including some of the founders, whose business or profession kept them from serving day-to-day. The board began to consider over-all neighborhood issues (rent gouging, stimulating local small business, urban renewal, representation on city agencies).

Basic council policy is decided by a governing assembly to which both the block-branches and the member institutions send delegates. Because the block-branches predominate, policy tends to express the opinions of the membership at large. The council's daily tasks are co-ordinated by an executive committee of elected officers and committee chairmen responsible to the assembly.

The overriding fear in Clinton Hill is that the bulldozer will wipe out the carefully nurtured community spirit, that declining facilities will impel public-spirited residents to move out. Some leaders have moved, but new ones have stepped forward. The chief hope is that neighborhood solidarity will deter powerful interests from aiding or abetting Clinton Hill's decay and instead foster its rejuvenation.

Outsiders find it difficult to fathom the Clinton Hill "spirit." The council employs no paid staff, but its leaders devote many hours to its affairs. All meetings, save large conferences, are held in private homes and apartments. Religious institutions of all faiths make available office facilities and equipment.

Its petitions saved for community use a large tract which a super-market chain sought to purchase. City officials are well aware of the area's strong desire for improved services. Regular annual events include a clean-up drive, a birthday party-social, and an open com-munity conference. Recently the council's program in schools and housing was published in "The Clinton Hill Community News" (circu-lation 10,000), which was paid for by small business advertising, written by a volunteer staff, and distributed free.

If the spontaneity, diversity, and independence of neighborhood councils were snuffed out, the results would be disheartening. Sterile paternalism would clog a potentially broad channel for genuine citizen involvement. The ability of the fringe areas to resist being burdened with much of the social and economic costs of urban redevelopment would be weakened. An imbalance in the urban decision-making process, already marked, would become irrevocable. By bringing to-gether whites and Negroes, small businessmen, tenants and home-owners, the neighborhood councils can become vehicles for peaceful and constructive change in the large cities.[4]

Three neighborhood councils in Chicago have helped to establish better relations between Negroes and whites and to lay a basis for integrated housing:

Neighborhood Change in Chicago, U.S.A.

The Lincoln Park Conservation Association had 600 dues-paying members in 1959. They took an affirmative action in reference to integrated housing for Negroes and whites by enacting: "Be it resolved that the Association, through example and intelligent planning, supply the ingredients to preserve our community and its surroundings as decent and desirable places in which sound family living is possible in a social climate appealing to men and women of goodwill regardless of race, color, or creed." They have to counteract fear that Negroes may become the dominant group, and the false propaganda of real estate speculators urging whites to "get out now."

The Chatham-Avalon-Park Community Council began with less than 100 members. At first Negroes did not join. By 1958 the membership had grown to over 500. Its school committee got more funds from the Board of Education for a program of human relations in the public schools. The organization also got the Chicago City Council to appropriate for a park.

The Winneconia Lake Area Improvement Association has prevented acts of violence against Negroes who have moved into the area. One member testified: "The Association takes in anyone and dissuades them or outvotes them after public discussion." However, members feel that a moderate quota should be set, lest Negroes become the dominant group. Others are concerned because whites do not get to know Negroes of their own cultural level.[5]

How may a community council undermine the customary pattern of community leadership?

A community council organized in a rural community in Brazil came to an end after two years for reasons thus explained by an anthropologist supplied by the United States:

Chonin de Cima, Brazil

Brazilian rural communities, as a rule, are organized along paternalistic, authoritarian lines, leadership being vested in family heads, priests, landowning patrons and political chiefs. Informal leadership tends to follow the same pattern. The Community Council constituted a break in the traditional lines of authority. Through it the local co-ordinator was able to dictate and to undermine the customary pattern of individual leadership. Greater success could have been achieved by first using the traditional form of leadership and by forming the Community Council only after concrete community interests had appeared demanding community action.

The Council included eight to ten leading members of the community selected so as to represent farmers, shopkeepers, craftsmen and housewives, and was nonpolitical in character. The local co-ordinator was an ex-schoolmaster lacking in leadership. Later he was succeeded by an agricultural technician who lacked tact and understanding.[6]

Note that the co-ordinators were specialists. Does this tend to prove our assertion (in Chapter V above) that "few such experts possess the social skills to win the co-operation of the citizens; working with people is a special art in itself; relatively few technical experts have this skill"? The anthropologist ascribes the collapse of the project to the failure to follow the customary pattern of leadership. The eight to ten "farmers, shopkeepers, craftsmen, and housewives," all of whom were "non-political," seem to have been chosen to wrest control of the project from the "family heads, priests, landowning patrons and political chiefs" which would have been usual. Although there must be situations where such traditional, autocratic power ought to be supplanted for the welfare of the people yet we should remember the advice contained in the record of life in Karimpur, India, in Chapter II above, which we shall repeat here:

He who would help the village cannot afford to ignore the power of present leaders. If he sees little hope of securing justice or improved conditions through them and has sufficient financial support, he can replace them. But he must make the substitution complete. . . . Partial replacement is more doubtful and may prove harmful to those whom it aims to help. . . . Where co-operative societies have been introduced with the support of established leaders, their chances of success have been greater. . . .

Co-operation which includes rather than replaces existing leaders is more desirable if the leaders are willing to co-operate. By sharing with them what we have learned of community welfare, we can help them to a more altruistic application of their power. They cannot be expected to change from selfish motives to community interests immediately. But once they care for the well-being, rather than the subservience, of their dependents, they can do more than outsiders can hope to do.[7]

A neighborhood council came to grief in New York City under similar circumstances. Prior to World War II the Southside (this name is fictitious) Neighborhood Council had the reputation among social workers of being the most successful in the city. It was organized as a typical council of social agencies of that period. In other words it included representatives of all the settlement houses and churches in the area and of the district offices of the Community Service Society, the Catholic and Jewish Charities, and also delegates from the schools, the branch libraries, and other agencies in the fields of group work, casework, and public health. At this period in the United States there were few councils organized as recommended by Morris Eisenstein. The Southside Neighborhood Council had two great advantages. It tended to overcome undesirable competition among the social and health agencies of the neighborhood. Also it encouraged the agencies to plan jointly for the development of the area and therefore to plan more wisely.

However, this Council had two chief weaknesses. There was little or no representation from the local residents of the district and therefore the planning was paternalistic rather than co-operative with those to be helped. Furthermore, this Council—like most councils of social agencies at this time, in most American cities—lacked prestige, and therefore was not effective in getting its plans carried out. Influential citizens who wielded financial and political influence were not intimately involved, and hence the council's deliberations were ineffective except on a very limited scale. Such councils had the reputation among politicians and businessmen of being organizations for "women, ministers, and social workers."

When the United States entered the war in 1941, the national Office of Civilian Defense, of which Mrs. Roosevelt was associate director, encouraged the formation of civilian defense councils, neighborhood councils, and even block councils and house councils in congested areas of apartment-house life. Everyone wanted to contribute to the war effort, and taking part in such councils eased the sense of frustration which most citizens felt who could not enter the armed forces. Where neighborhood councils already existed they were expanded and enlarged in membership. Local businessmen and politicians joined the Southside Neighborhood Council and took an active part in all its deliberations. Effort had been made to include all organized groups. No political group could afford to stay out. At last the Council became a potent instrument for expressing the will of the neighborhood.

When the war ended, most of the house councils and block councils fell apart, lacking the war spirit which had energized them. The Southside Neighborhood Council, however, faced growing pains. Formerly, the social workers had had matters all their own way, but not any more. Local residents active in business and in politics had now found personal satisfaction in Council meetings and had been elected to office and been active on committees. An issue arose which divided the membership. The local residents wished to organize a Fourth-of-July parade similar to some of the wartime demonstrations which had been so popular. The professional social workers, who had formerly dominated the Council, felt that such a parade was a foolish waste of energy, but they were outvoted and the parade was held. It had publicity value for the Council which might easily have been transformed into the type of neighbors' council recommended by Morris Eisenstein, had the professional workers been willing to co-operate, but they and their sponsoring agencies withdrew their support. The last information I have is that the Southside Neighborhood Council has come to an end, and that no successor has been organized.

*   *   *

Summary. Community councils are needed to build unity and prevent distracting competition among agencies. Such councils can promote joint planning for the welfare of the community. In large cities, neighborhood councils representing the rank and file of citizens are desirable. By stimulating citizen co-operation and self-help they assist in urban development on a co-operative rather than a paternalistic basis. Care should be taken to include the customary leaders in the council, where that is possible. Efforts to undermine the customary pattern of community leadership are likely to fail.

VIII. TRAINING

How to provide field work training for new community workers

If you are now an experienced community worker you may be asked to train new workers. I strongly urge you to seek this opportunity for two reasons. In the first place, because of the great need in the world today for more workers skilled in stimulating and guiding community action. There is hardly a nation that does not need hundreds or even thousands more of these workers. In a country like India the number of village-level workers needed is simply astronomical.

A second reason why you should seek an opportunity to train others is for your own growth. No one thoroughly learns a thing until he has tried to teach it to someone else. The experience will take time and effort, but it will consolidate your own understanding of the art in which you are engaged, and teach you things about yourself that you did not know. This difficult art cannot be readily taught by a lecture in the classroom. Like any other art it must be learned by *doing*. In schools of social work in the United States this is attempted by what is known as "field work." The student leaves the classroom and spends a large portion of his time working with people in a community, under the guidance of an experienced community worker. The student should do more than *observe* how his teacher works. As far as possible (although this is not easy) the student himself should become involved, and should actually help his teacher, if only in mechanical ways. The student should actually be *understudying* the work of his chief. He should be always closely associated with the latter and should go along wherever his chief goes.

In the first field-work arrangement in which I served as supervisor, a vigorous young man known as "Mac" was assigned to me full time for three months. For this he was to receive so many points of credit at the school of social work, and from the experience he hoped to draw material for his master's thesis. Although he worked hard in my office and in the community we paid him nothing. I explained to my president and to our board of directors that in return he must be allowed to sit in on all conferences, no matter how confidential, and should be entitled to accompany me wherever I went. He hoped to become the executive of a community council or united community fund, like myself. (However, the last I heard of him, the governor of his home state had appointed him State Commissioner of Public Welfare.)

One of the first jobs Mac helped me with was getting ready for a large meeting by borrowing chairs from a nearby church. Our organization had a slender budget, and little furniture, although we had been loaned a large empty meeting room. Mac and I got into my old station wagon, went after the chairs, brought them to the meeting room, and later returned them to the church. I had been teaching at the school of social work and Mac had been one of my students. I remember that the second or third time when we had to borrow chairs for a meeting Mac said to me as we were unloading them: "You didn't tell us in the course in community organization that one of the main jobs of a community organizer was hauling and arranging chairs!"

Mac helped me in other ways that were not so mechanical. Hardly a day passed when we did not have some committee meeting. Mac always took notes as secretary of the meeting. Even when I was able to have a stenographer present, he took notes also, and supervised the stenographer in producing the final minutes. I required him to keep a "diary"—not actually every day—sometimes recording important matters more than once a day, sometimes only every two or three days. In it he recorded his own thoughts about what had happened and questions he wished to ask me. I read his diary every few days, as he produced it, and learned a good deal about my own performances from his record. Once, I remember, I had been under great strain and I lost my temper with one of my own board members in a meeting. (Fortunately for me he was a broad-minded person, admitted his mistake when I had made my apologies, and we became lifelong friends.) However, the whole occurrence went down in Mac's record. If one takes on such a relationship with a student, he must be prepared to let him see his mistakes and failures as well as his successes.

For the best results for the student, frequent informal conferences are desirable. He must not be seated in some secluded corner, given "busy work" and then have a formal conference once a week with his busy chief. In all community work there are frequent unexpected emergencies. For the student these occurrences often contain the best educational material. It is desirable but extremely difficult that as soon as a peaceful moment ensues, his supervisor should explain to the student the inner significance of the occurrence, and the lessons to be drawn from it.

How to train new community workers by discussion of case material

You may be asked to teach a *group* of prospective community workers. If so I strongly urge you to use the *discussion* method, not to *lecture* to them.

A few years ago I received a letter from an international expert in the training of village-level workers. He had just returned from the Far East. He said in part:

Almost without exception, village workers are trained in agriculture, co-operatives, cottage industry, adult literacy, home economics, and in other "content" fields of instruction. While there is widespread under-standing of the need to train workers to help villagers acquire attitudes, concepts, and skills of effective participation in community problem solving, i.e., *the process of working with people in programs of planned change,* little or nothing is done about it. In effect, the training of multipurpose extension workers is confined to the technical skills. . . . The case study method is a relatively new one in the underde-veloped countries. The threat that seems to be implied to trainers who depart from the traditional lecture method to do more creative teach-ing seems to be as great in these countries as it is on American campuses.[1]

In most large universities in the United States undergraduates are instructed in large classes by the lecture method. The student takes notes which he later endeavors to memorize so as to pass the final examination. Unfortunately little of this information remains in the student's mind a few months later. Perhaps a thoroughly documented science can be imparted to large classes by the lecture method, but not the art of working with people in communities. No one has yet deduced from it a dependable set of scientific principles which can be imparted to students. If we are ever to arrive at a science of community development, we shall have to derive the principles by analyzing case material. This is excellent training for students. As early as possible they must learn by doing. This may be approximated by inspiring them to analyze com-munity case records in small discussion groups in which they take an active part. From these records, and from their own imaginative thinking, they can seek a vicarious experience.

After some ten years of community work I had the good fortune to be invited to teach community organization at the New York School of Social Work (now a graduate department of Columbia

University). It was the policy of the School to limit the size of classes to seminar groups of not more than thirty students, so that each student might feel a responsibility for taking an active part in class discussion. No effort was made to cram into the student's head a vast amount of information which he would memorize from lecture notes. The effort was rather to stimulate him to think for himself about community problems which he might expect to meet later in his practice. There was no assumption that the instructor had the final answer to such problems, but rather that the class and the instructor were engaged in a joint effort to discover certain lessons to be learned by analyzing together case situations which had confronted other workers like themselves.

I employed this same method at Tulane University, and again in a Seminar on Community Development jointly sponsored by Haverford College and the United Nations, on the Haverford campus. One advantage of the method was that discussion of a dynamic case seemed to awaken interest more keenly than a formal lecture.

It has been wisely said that education begins with interest. Those who teach by the case method are not attempting primarily to transmit information, but rather to stimulate interest, so that the student will seek information for himself. The instructor can supply the source material. True education is self-education.

Drawing fundamental lessons from the experience of others in working with people in a community, and suggesting what one would do in like circumstances, forces the student to reconsider his own basic philosophy of working with people. The necessity for arriving at such basic conclusions for himself is perhaps the most important advantage of the case method. The student may never face the exact difficulty portrayed in the case record, but if he is led to a sound philosophy of working with any people anywhere, it will stand him in good stead wherever he goes.

Discussion of case material is time consuming. It should not be attempted by an instructor who feels a compulsion to "cover the subject." It is better to relax and be content to provoke thought and stimulate mental growth, knowing that in a limited number of sessions it is impossible to exhaust and impart all the information you possess. If you are skillful in awakening the student to think for himself, he will retain far more than if he had taken notes and memorized a formal lecture.

Good teaching is an art. Each instructor must discover by trial and error the method which is best for him. The suggestions which follow illustrate how I would endeavor to use a typical case. No other instructor would use it in exactly the same way.

Let us select the case from Ocampo, Mexico, quoted in Chapter II above. If you or I were using this material in a training center in India or the Philippines, for example, we might mimeograph the part contained in Chapter II and distribute it to our class.

The sequel and the analysis appearing on later pages would be held back, and the students encouraged to seek their own solution of the difficulty, and make their own analysis. The sequel (see the beginning of Chapter III) would be given them orally later.

This mimeographed record would be distributed to the class at least a day before it was to be discussed. Before the class met, the instructor would place on the blackboard certain key questions, suggested by the text, to stimulate thought, such as these:

1. How can outsiders avoid being sponsored by the wrong group?
2. How do outsiders discover what the community wants?
3. When are outsiders necessary or desirable?

If no blackboard is available the instructor will have to invent a substitute, perhaps mounting the questions on a sheet of wrapping paper pinned to the wall. A rough map could also be drawn, showing the location of the city, and the village, river, footbridge, highway, church, school, and other factors related to the case. It might even be worth while to draw a simple organization chart showing the interrelation of the American Friends Service Committee in Philadelphia, the Friends Headquarters in Mexico City, and the local Friends Service Unit in the village, as well as the National Government at Mexico City, the Governor of the State, the *Agente* of the City of Ocampo, and the citizens of the village. The purpose of all this is to give the students something visible on which to focus their attention as they discuss the record, and to make the situation more real to them.

The questions on the board should provoke thought and be *generic*; that is, they should apply not only to this community and this situation, but to any future situation in which the student may find himself.

For at least the first five or ten minutes of the session the instructor should expect to use the lecture technique. If he knows the community well he may describe it in more detail, or tell small anecdotes about it, to bring the situation more to life. For instance, the fact that the men among the Friends wore homemade sandals like the villagers, and that all the girls wore skirts in deference to convention, although in the United States they would frequently have gone about in slacks. Almost at once the instructor may pose the debatable question of to what extent one should yield to local custom in community work. Should a Protestant attend the Catholic Church, et cetera. The instructor thus endeavors as early as possible to break down the student's diffidence and accustom him to take part in discussion.

If there is any possibility of introducing a note of humor, the time for it is in this introduction. For example, when I visited this Mexican village and was introduced to the young Friends, I noticed one of the young men who was swarthy wore long sideburns like a Spanish bullfighter. I presumed him to be Mexican, but found that he was a boy from Yonkers, a suburban city near New York. To many people the name "Yonkers" has a humorous connotation. As the joke in this case was on the instructor, I have used this episode in order to relax the students at the beginning, and to break down the psychological distance that exists between instructor and students, and build up a feeling that all are engaged together in the enterprise of searching for dependable lessons in community development to be drawn from the case material.

I have been assuming that the session at which Ocampo is being considered is at least the second, or a later period in the course, and that it may be possible after the first five or ten minutes to get the students talking at least to the extent of asking questions. At the first session of the course the introduction will have to be longer. The instructor may have to lecture for a whole hour, although this should be avoided if possible. There are several devices which can be used. Almost at the beginning the truth should be impressed upon the students that each brings to the class a contribution all his own. Every community, like every individual, has its own personality. The students come from different communities, and each should be urged to show the peculiar characteristics of his town in relation to the discussion in the class. One way to get the students started taking an active part is to go around the class asking each student where he comes from, the size of the town, and perhaps other peculiarities of his community.

Do not spend much time in the first hour of the course in definitions. They are dull, and of little help when one comes to active practice. Instead of a long definition of "community development," give them at the start an example of a problem in community development. This may be done orally, as a short case record, and if skillfully used can start the class on active participation, discussing a debatable issue raised by the case.

I prefer a two-hour session with a ten-minute intermission in the middle. Occasionally I have found it possible to issue a simple mimeographed record like "Ocampo" for them to read during the intermission, and thus get started on the discussion of a specific case during the second hour. Even for the first introductory session of the course there should be, if possible, specific provocative questions on the board on which the students can focus their attention when they first enter the room.

To get started on the first of the three questions listed above in connection with the Ocampo case record, the instructor may give two or three other illustrations of the same difficulty. It might be well to ask members of the class whether they have ever observed similar difficulties in communities in which they have lived.

The instructor will sense intuitively at what point the first question has served its educative purpose sufficiently, and it is time to pass on to the next. When the class has struggled with the problem of how too close affiliation with the Senator's party might have been avoided, the instructor may tell the class about the meeting at the schoolhouse, described in Chapter III, and how victory was eventually wrested from defeat.

Case material consisting of a simple success story is seldom as educational as one illustrating a realistic difficulty and how it was overcome. Even a failure may make excellent teaching material if the reason for the failure is clear and a lesson can be drawn from it, helpful to the students.

When I first used the discussion method with case material I feared that we might run out of material for useful discussion before the two-hour session was over. Instead, I found that there was seldom time to consider all that might be usefully discussed in connection with the two or three questions placed on the board as the agenda for the session. However, the instructor should have on a sheet of paper before him a well-worked-out plan for presenting further material if time permits. He may present additional case material or an interesting and pertinent anecdote, or perhaps direct the class in considering that age-old and related question—How can the outsider steer a wise course between contending political forces?—with accounts of success or failure stated and analyzed by both the instructor and members of the class.

In theory at least, the session should end with a succinct summary of the conclusions reached, and of the different points of view expressed during the day's discussion. I am not good at this difficult art of summarizing. I have usually rationalized this defect by stressing that productive discussion was still going on with intense interest until time for adjournment. However, I do believe in the value of such a summary. Occasionally I have been able to delegate the summary to a capable student. The effort to summarize the day's discussion is a valuable educational experience.

At the conclusion of the session the instructor will, of course, tell the class of any sequel to the case record which he has held back as a device for stimulating class discussion. In doing so he will endeavor to make clear the lessons to be drawn from the case.

I have an antipathy to the usual written examination. As a rule it shows ability to memorize, rather than ability to think for oneself. In nearly every class, however, there are thoughtful but silent members who do not show their real abilities in competition with more vocal students.

For this and several other reasons students should be urged at the beginning of the course to search their memories and life experience for an occurrence which they can put on paper as case material illustrating some problem in community development. The search for such an episode, difficult as that search may be, is educative. Frequently the difficulty is to isolate a simple problem from a complicated and confused mass of facts. The student should be asked to describe briefly the community in which the problem arose, and then to state and analyze the problem. Sometimes it may be an issue which has not yet arisen, but may validly be anticipated. Again a simple success story is less to be desired than one illustrating realistic difficulties akin to those which may face members of the class in their later practice.

It has been my custom to choose two of the best student papers and, with permission of the authors, mimeograph them and issue them to the class for discussion at the last two sessions of the course. In this connection, the *best* paper does not mean the one which is best written, but rather the episode which will lend itself most readily to class discussion; which has the most educational value, or which rounds out the course by illustrating some problem which has thus far not been adequately dealt with. Such student papers may prove the best teaching material of the course. Because the issue is raised by one of their own number, the material usually seems more realistic, and is more interesting to the class than anything the instructor can bring to them. If the issue is a current one which the student will face when he returns to his community, he should be warned that he may not get a ready-made answer to his problem, either from the class or from the instructor. On one occasion I had in my class a field group organizer on leave from the Division of Community Education of Puerto Rico. He wrote a stimulating paper portraying some of the difficulties he would face in interpreting the work of his Division when he returned to the island. In effect he taught the class that day, and I sat with the students. He had followed my custom and had placed three or four provocative questions on the board before us. For the first half hour he was kept busy answering our questions as to the peculiarities of the community, supplementing what he had given us in his paper. Then I had to call a halt on asking that type of question. It was evident that the class felt inadequate to cope with the fundamental questions he wished us to come to grips with, and was postponing this difficult task by continuing to ask more questions about the setting.

At last we set ourselves to struggle with his problems, such as to what extent the parish priest would be an asset or an obstacle in his work; how to overcome the handicap of only a few citizens being able to read, but gathering each afternoon at the local store to hear the newspaper read aloud; and so on and so on. Soon our time was up and we had to adjourn. Afterward in congratulating the student on how well he had conducted the session, I asked him whether he felt that he had wasted his time. The discussion had been educational for the class and for the instructor, but with his greater knowledge of the community he had shown us that few of the courses of action which we had suggested would have proved practical. He replied that on the contrary, as he had analyzed the situation for us he had come to a much clearer understanding of what he would face when he returned to his District, and had determined in his own mind just what action he would undertake.

If you have had considerable community experience, you will be able to write your own community case record and give it to the class. You will not need to use the Ocampo record, or perhaps any other record written by others. If you have actually taken part in the situation yourself, you can make it real to the class, can tell them more about the community and can lead them to sound conclusions with confidence because the case is *yours*.

*   *   *

Summary. New community workers can best be trained by supervised field work and by group discussion of case material. The field work student should keep a diary, and he should have frequent informal conferences with his supervisor. Analysis of case material in small groups is far better than formal lectures. The aim should be stimulation of thought about realistic problems rather than the imparting of voluminous information.

IX. OTHER PROBLEMS OF COMMUNITY ACTION

How to work with the people as their colleague rather than as a superior expert

You will remember that in the Northern Territories of the Gold Coast (Chapter III above) the new community development workers (instead of acting superior like the former district officers) actually worked with the villagers in digging the holes for latrines and helping to pour the cement. As a result the villagers accepted their instructions, and the latrines did not remain unused as formerly.

Dalip S. Saund, who was born in India, but served as a United States Congressman from California, visited a Philippine village and reported as follows:

Calloused Hands in the Philippines

At one barrio I was much impressed by the personality of a college graduate who had been assigned the task of organizing and assisting the community. We met the leaders of the community at the com-

munity center which had been constructed under the supervision of
this young man. He showed us his hands, calloused from working
alongside the villagers. He clearly had won the affection of the people
there. I was quite amazed and astonished because the oriental educated
class has traditionally been afraid of doing any physical labor. Here
was a brilliant and successful exception![1]

In the island of Puerto Rico an excellent program for com-
munity development is carried on by group organizers under the
Division of Community Education. An example is the work of
Zacarias Rodriguez described in Chapter IV above.

I wrote the director of the Division asking how his excellent
staff was selected and what experience or training they had before
he appointed them. Here is a paragraph from his reply:

> We did not set out to choose fishermen and farmers, preachers and
> policemen, teachers and health inspectors. That is just what they hap-
> pened to be doing when we discovered the depth of their hearts. Of
> course, among the 1,500 we interviewed during that initial 18-month
> period back in 1949–50, there were many "professionals." And some
> made it, but not many, for we discovered an interesting thing about
> them. The more "professional" they were the less they wanted *to work
> with people*. They wanted to work "once removed." They wanted to
> *work with those who work with people*.

If you are working in a large city, seeking to stimulate an urban
neighborhood to community action, the phrase "working with
people" may not mean physical co-operation. It will probably
mean sharing their problems intellectually as Jane Addams did at
Hull House in Chicago. But if you work in a rural community,
particularly in what is called an "underdeveloped" country, you
can and should work with them in actual physical exertion.

Rosulia Rural Center, India

In 1951 the American Friends Service Committee, in collaboration
with British Quakers, was operating a Rural Center at Rosulia in

Madya Pradesh, India. They felt it desirable, as an experiment, to add to their Western staff of technicians and specialists two young American men who would be assigned to work alongside the people of the village on local self-help projects. These men were carefully selected. While they had no specialty or technical training, they had grown up on farms, had practical mechanical skills, and had had some college training. They had sought an opportunity for service abroad with Friends, and as conscientious objectors to war were fulfilling their alternate service under the United States draft law.

During their period of service, in addition to general construction work, they assisted in the dairy and helped develop, locally, simple mechanical tools and agricultural implements. By actually sharing in the manual work of village projects, such as well digging and road building, these young men stimulated greater village participation and helped the people to sustain their enthusiasm and effort, and to complete projects. They became close friends of the young Indians on the Rural Center staff. Because these American men came not as teachers or "experts" but as manual workers, and lived and worked as equals of the people of the villages, they were able to gain the villagers' confidence and to share intimately in discussions of the problems and implications of democracy and of the changing social pattern, with which the younger Indians were struggling. (Even in depressed urban centers, such as parts of Philadelphia, the American Friends Service Committee has succeeded in organizing "weekend work camps" in which college students and other young volunteers work side by side with local residents on self-help projects to physically improve slum neighborhoods.)[2]

Do not assume from my use of these illustrations that I am insisting that you also must necessarily engage in well digging or cement work. (Perhaps you're not very good at pouring cement!) What I *am* insisting is that in your own best judgment and your own way you shall establish a relationship with the people among whom you work so that they come to regard you as working *with* them (not *for* them) and certainly not as one whom they must regard as their superior.

The Pilot Project, established in Etawah in Uttar Pradesh, India, mentioned in Chapter V, was initiated by Albert Mayer, with the aid of Horace Holmes. Both are internationally famous experts—Mayer as a town planner, and Holmes as an agriculturist. Yet they were not above holding the handle of an improved plow to show how to use it, or digging the holes for tree planting or soakage pits. One of Mayer's first bulletins to his fellow workers contained this paragraph:

Our own attitudes as government workers are most crucial; we must work with people, not tell them; we must demonstrate by doing with our own hands in their own villages and fields—in short, "dirty hands" methods, not "armchair" methods.

Is the role of women in community action different from the role of men?

Except for a few minor pros and cons, the answer to this question is "No." Do not assume that women are even precluded from taking active part physically in self-help activities. Sometimes women even bear a major share of the burden:

South Volta, Ghana

Nine villages in the South Volta region in Ghana were short of water. A government engineer worked out plans for a rain-pool that would supply the water needed. There was delay in government action and the rainy season was approaching. Following the plans designed by the engineer, thirty women and eighteen men built the pool. The women carried the earth on their heads in baskets or trays.[3]

In many cultures the status of women in the community is so low that community planners tend to overlook them, thereby making a sad mistake. A famous example of this occurred in New Mexico:

Hybrid Corn in New Mexico, U.S.A.

The county agent's relations with the farmers were good. He spoke Spanish in the same manner, was familiar with their background and agricultural practices, and had served as agent for several years immediately preceding this venture. The seed corn, he felt, had degenerated and he suspected this was an important factor in keeping production low. He decided to introduce a hybrid seed that was known for high yield, and proceeded carefully, consulting with the college agronomist, who selected a variety—Hybrid U.S. 30—that had been tested in the immediate area. It was considered disease-resistant and capable of producing a good growth, averaging 100 bushels to the acre.

Then the agent discussed the problem of low corn yields with the leaders of the village, having chosen this particular community as a likely place for a good response. The men readily recognized the need for better production and were willing to think that, perhaps, their seed strain was weakening after long continuous propagation.

The soils of the fields used by this village were tested and found to be of good fertility, since here, as elsewhere in the area, it had been customary to use some manure yearly. After discussion with the leaders of the various problems involved, a meeting was called in order to present the county agent's plan.

Everyone in the village was invited to the meeting. The agent showed movies of the hybrid corn, and cartoons, to enliven the demonstration. Then the leaders took over the meeting and explained in their own words the plan for introducing hybrid corn. All those present seemed to agree that the new seed was the answer to many of their problems, and that they would be well able to afford the price of the seed, once it was available locally.

By special arrangement with a grower of seed, the new hybrid was furnished in exchange for the old seed. A demonstration plot which clearly showed a triple crop was set up near the village, with the result that 40 farmers planted hybrid and each doubled his production the first year.

The whole procedure seemed to have been soundly based and to have got unusually rapid results. There was confirmation of this when, in the following year, the county agent was able to report that 60 farmers, about three-fourths of all the growers in the village, had accepted the new seed.

However, two years later this apparent success had turned to failure. In 1948 although the high yield had continued, only 30 farmers planted hybrid. The other 30 who had planted it the year before went back to the traditional variety. The next year, 1949, only three farmers planted hybrid corn. Furthermore, none of the farmers in neighboring villages had changed to the higher yielding seed, as the agent had hoped they would. Inquiring as to why the farmers had all gone back to planting the low-yield native corn, he finally discovered the answer.

All the wives had complained. Some did not like its texture; it did not hang together well for tortillas; the tortillas were not the color of mixtamal (the corn flour dough to which they were accustomed). Few had cared for the flavor, but the farmers who persisted in planting it after the first year had hoped that they would get used to it. It made abundant food for the stock and they were reluctant to drop it for that reason.[4]

Please note that here the community worker showed great skill in at least six particulars. (1) He spoke the language of the people and understood their customs (except for the recipe for tortillas). (2) He first consulted an agronomist. (3) He discussed the matter first with a small group of leaders (the "snowball" technique). (4) Then he organized a meeting of the entire community. (5) The leaders "took over" and explained the plan while he kept silent (indirect leadership). (6) He arranged to have one farmer plant a "demonstration plot."

The only thing he forgot was to consult the housewives. Were they present at the community meeting? We are told that "everyone in the village was invited." Perhaps it would have been foreign to the Mexican-Indian custom for the women to speak up if they had any doubts about the new plan.

I can think of only one other thing which the county agent might have done to save the situation. He might have consulted in advance with another specialist. Undoubtedly there was in that

county a woman "home demonstration agent" trained to serve the
housewives as the county agricultural agent was trained to serve
the farmers. She would have known all about the making of tortillas and might have questioned whether "Hybrid U.S. 30," although better for the stock, might be unpalatable as human food.
Indeed, had she been consulted before the people had lost confidence in the county agent, a compromise might have been worked
out. Some of the new Hybrid seed might have been planted for the
stock, and some of the former seed might still have been grown for
making tortillas.

Let us not conclude from this instance that women are more
conservative than men in accepting constructive change. Indeed
there is much more evidence to the contrary. Here is an instance
from Spain:

Land Titles in Western Spain

In the western part of Spain it was traditional for land to be divided
by inheritance until few farmers had sufficient acreage to support a
family. Let us suppose a grandfather owned 40 acres and had 4 sons,
each of whom had 4 sons (to make the mathematics simple). Each
grandson would inherit only 2½ acres, because their fathers would
each receive only 10 acres on the grandfather's death. Finally parcels
became so fractional that a local joke was told of one owner who could
not find his land because he had cast down his overcoat over it.

The community development man worked out a plan for land
reform without expropriation or legislation. He worked out a plan for
trading land so that each farmer would receive enough adjoining
parcels to constitute a farm large enough to support a family. The men
of the district proved to be bound by tradition, or too jealous lest some
other farmers get more than they did. The plan seemed defeated until
the community worker dealt with the farmers' wives, when the men's
objections were overcome and the plan adopted.[5]

This suggests to me an issue that arose in Madison, Wisconsin,
when I was in high school. Our high school building was old and

overcrowded. Temporary schoolrooms were fixed up in the gable ends of the attic. The entire attic was not floored over. Improvised sidewalks were constructed on which we passed from one class-room to another. On either side of the sidewalk there was nothing but the lath and plaster ceiling of the rooms below. We boys used to try to push each other off the sidewalk. It was delightful to imagine what would happen if, someday, someone broke through the ceiling.

Sure enough, one day it happened! As some of us were pretend-ing to study in the large study hall below, a girl, passing from an attic recitation room, stepped off the sidewalk, and a leg appeared, projecting through the ceiling above us. We students were much amused, and went home and told our parents about it gleefully. Our mothers were not amused. They resolved that we should have a new high school building. Our fathers protested that taxes were too high; the city could not afford it. Woman suffrage had not yet arrived, but women could vote in school matters. When the vote was taken the women and the young men (who had suffered in the old building) carried the day against the old men who had ruled the town economically. A bond issue was contested by the latter in the courts, but the issue was upheld, and the new building was built.

In most communities in the United States women have more leisure time than men. They are therefore very active in united community fund drives and many other forms of community action related to social work. In the "Colored Problems Study" in Medford (see Chapter VI above) the Women's Club played an effective and unexpected role.

Medford Community
Self-Study, U.S.A. (*continued*)

As the Medford [Community Self-Study] went on, Miss Radborne was much in demand to speak before various civic and church groups.

She was a modest but courageous person with a frank and pleasing delivery. The climax was reached when she was asked to speak before the Medford Women's Club. This was the most fashionable and influential society in town. The wives and daughters of the dominant male leaders in commerce, finance, and industry belonged to it. At the close of the meeting, after Miss Radborne had explained the purpose and method of the study, there were many questions. A great deal of interest was shown, and after the meeting the president of the club asked Miss Radborne how they could help. She offered the services of forty members of the club who would be willing to volunteer half-time for two weeks! Miss Radborne came back to the office and conferred with Miss Ibsen and myself. We had wanted citizen participation, but were we prepared to make use of forty volunteers, the cream of Medford's "400"?

The most appropriate area seemed to be the Housing Committee. Miss Ibsen and Miss Radborne went to New York and interviewed a housing expert on the staff of the Russell Sage Foundation. He asked whether these women were housewives who could be relied upon to inspect tenements and report whether they were in good repair, whether they were clean, filthy, or in between, etc., etc. He finally agreed to prepare a simple set of inspection cards on which these volunteers could check their findings. And then the work began! For two weeks these forty women tramped up and down the outside wooden stairways of the ancient tenements along Richmond Street. The area was only six blocks away from my office, but I had never been there, and I am sure no one from the Women's Club had either, although the property was owned by their husbands and brothers. The quarters were not fit for human habitation, yet most of our Negro and Italian citizens had to live there. The Women's Club was shocked. They held an indignation meeting and resolved to make the removal of such conditions their chief endeavor even if "it took two years!"

Meanwhile I confess I was getting worried. The United Community Fund was about to start its campaign. It supported the Community Council and the Study. Would the male leadership of the town turn against us? They owned the newspaper. When would the city editor phone me that he could no longer co-operate with us? That call never came. The paper published in sections the entire final report of the Committee, with many drastic findings and recommendations. The Fund made its goal without difficulty. Why? "Never underestimate the power of a woman!"

Today those wooden tenements are gone. It took more than the two years, but the modern brick low-cost housing areas where the Negroes and Italians live are, at least in part, due to the Community Self-Study and the forty volunteers.[6]

How can the emotional needs of a community leader become a constructive force?

There lived in Medford a famous Negro woman lecturer and writer who presented a serious problem when we were organizing the Central Committee [of the Self-Study]. Everyone who knew her said that we could not possibly have her on the Committee. She had been spoiled by a great deal of adulation from white citizens, and could not work in a group. She would insist on dominating the Committee. Yet she was the most prominent Negro citizen in Medford and had lived there longer than most Negroes.

Miss Radborne succeeded in solving this difficulty. She asked this distinguished person if (although too busy with writing and lecturing to attend a lot of committee meetings) she would help by writing the introduction to the Report. She, better than anyone else, knew the historic facts as to why and how Negroes commenced coming to Medford. She could describe how this immigration continued, and she had the ability as a writer to set forth this first chapter of the Report. The author agreed and did an excellent job. Her name signed to the introduction gave prestige to the Report, and at no time was she any obstacle to the study.

Perhaps few people realize that many social agencies have come into being less because of a felt need in the community than because of the emotional needs of the organizer. Here is an example:

Mrs. Taylor and the
Fairhaven Travelers Aid, U.S.A.

Mrs. Taylor, the founder of the Travelers Aid in Fairhaven, was the wife of a well-to-do dentist. She was a person of great energy and executive ability. She had no children. Her husband was docile and easily managed. She had spent most of her energy as program chairman of the women's club of her church, which sponsored a Sunday night forum. In seeking a speaker for this forum she learned that a field secretary of the National Travelers Aid Society would be available. Mrs. Taylor had no special interest in Travelers Aid but she wanted a good speaker. The field secretary proved excellent. She made a most stirring appeal, and explained that Fairhaven as a railroad and truck center with 150,000 population should have such a service. She painted a sad picture of the fate of some young woman who might find herself stranded at the Fairhaven station that night. Mrs. Taylor vibrated with interest. Still kindled with excitement, she drove the speaker down to the station and put her on the night train. Most of the night she lay awake making plans.

She was at the station early the next morning and bulldozed the station master into setting aside a corner of the station for her use. She borrowed an old desk from her husband's office. She persuaded a friend of her husband, who owned a truck, to move the desk to the station, and by 10:30 Tuesday morning the Fairhaven Travelers Aid was born! It was as simple as that. There was a little delay in getting a telephone, but with Mrs. Taylor's energy all things were possible. She spent all of every day at the station. She *was* the Travelers Aid. But even she had to leave the station for lunch or to do things for her clients. (When she got hold of a "case" she hung on to it; she didn't "refer" it.) Finally she admitted another woman to the partnership, a co-worker in her church club. For some time they financed their work with what money Mrs. Taylor could secure from her husband. But more funds were needed. Mrs. Taylor went through the form of organizing a society with a board. The president was a manufacturer who was a member of her church. She herself was vice-president. The board never met, but contributed money. About this time a Community Chest was formed in Fairhaven. I became the executive of the Chest and the Council of Social Agencies. All the other agencies in the Council complained that there was a lack of standards in the Travelers Aid, and that Mrs. Taylor did not co-operate or refer. She in turn alleged that the social workers in the various agencies were inhuman and hard-boiled. All the other agencies had salaried workers paid with money furnished by the Chest. Reluctantly Mrs. Taylor accepted a small salary. Finally the executive of the National Travelers Aid Association was called in. When he insisted that Mrs. Taylor must either resign as a salaried worker or as a vice-president, she remained vice-president and a trained social worker was employed.

A few weeks later Mrs. Taylor came in to consult the Council of Social Agencies on the need for an old people's home in Fairhaven. I explained that there was an old men's home and two old women's homes. "But you see," said Mrs. Taylor, "there is no home for old couples." She was fairly patient with me while I explained that we would call a meeting of the Case Work Division to discuss the matter with her. They asked her to bring in a list of the couples who needed this service, and then adjourned for a week. Mrs. Taylor brought in a list of twelve couples. Their names were run through the Social Service Exchange. Ten of them were already under the care of social agencies in their own homes, but two couples were not known to any agency. Mrs. Taylor was gleeful. "Then you will help me build the old couples' home!" But the chairman of the committee explained that it would be better for the two couples (and less expensive) to find families that would board them than to build an institution for them. For a moment Mrs. Taylor was disheartened. "What a pity," she said, "for I already have an option on a wonderful piece of property in the West End, and you know Miss Brown, who has just been let out as superintendent of nurses at the hospital? She would make a wonderful matron."

Today there is an old people's home in Fairhaven on the plot in the West End, and Miss Brown is Matron. When Mrs. Taylor's plan was disapproved by the Council of Social Agencies, she went to the national headquarters of her church and proposed that the home be built as a national memorial to a famous hymn writer of that denomination, and that old couples from all over the nation might be sent to the home through their local churches. A skilled money-raising firm in New York was engaged. A national campaign was put on, and the building was built.

Obviously the chief motivation in establishing both these organizations was the need for an outlet for Mrs. Taylor's energies, rather than the community's need. Let us not belittle the Mrs. Taylors; they can be very useful. The sad thing is that professional social workers seldom have the skill to direct a Mrs. Taylor's drive into useful channels. Our tendency is to be negative, to tell her just to relax and let us do it. Well guided, a Mrs. Taylor can be more useful in community organization than any social worker. The greatest obstacle which the community organizer faces is community apathy and inertia. There is no apathy or inertia where the Mrs. Taylors are. Here is an example of a constructive use of a "Mrs. Taylor":

Standard Family Budget in Beechmont, U.S.A.

In Beechmont there was a Mrs. Jones who served on several social agency boards. She had had a little social work training, was married to a husband with a good income, and had no children. The executives of the agencies on whose boards she served complained that she was domineering and that she meddled in the administrative duties of the staff. For years she was a problem. Then the Council of Social Agencies organized a committee to devise a standard family budget for use by all relief agencies. Mrs. Jones accepted the chairmanship. She organized subcommittees on food, clothing, rent, and so forth. She drove herself, her committee and her subcommittees unmercifully. She brought to town a national expert on home economics to advise with the committee. Even her severest critics agreed that Mrs. Jones was proving to be one of the most useful citizens in town.

Emotional needs and frustrations produce activity on the part of both ourselves and others. To those who desire a quiet life or wish to maintain the status quo, such an emotional drive may seem an

unfavorable phenomenon. Well guided, it may result in over-
coming community apathy and produce constructive change.

When is it best for a volunteer community leader to speak?

When Miss Parker suggested that the chemical engineer should
present the case for a mental health clinic in Woodhurst (Chapter
IV) the main purpose was to get him more completely involved in
the movement. A secondary reason was that he was a recognized
conservative community leader whose sponsorship would carry
great weight. All too often in community meetings it is the voice of
the trained community worker which is heard, until the volunteer
members of the community tend to get tired of the repetition. He
therefore should consciously plan to get others to present the same
points when he can. This is also good indirect leadership, and gives
credit to others than himself. An early mistake on my part taught
me this forcibly.

Woodhurst Big Gifts Division, U.S.A.

The Community Chest in Woodhurst, of which I was executive,
started off well because it was a new idea. There were about 30,000
families in town, and after a few years we had secured 30,000 givers,
but the size of the gifts was small. Times were hard. The work of the
various agencies was growing rapidly and more money was needed
emergently. John Watson, a not too successful business man, had
volunteered at the start of the chest to head up the big gifts division.
He enjoyed approaching the most wealthy men in town for their
contributions. He himself gave $100 the first year and continued to
give the same amount each year with no increase. By the third annual
campaign we had reached a point of stagnation known to the professional money raisers as horizontal giving. Most of the men employed
in the factories contributed just a dollar bill. John Watson preached
that until the factory workers gave more, those in the big gifts division
could not be expected to give more. To a factory worker one dollar

was a more generous gift than $100 from John Watson. They made up their minds that until the "big boys" gave more they could not be expected to give two dollars, which would be doubling their gifts while those at the top continued to subscribe "horizontally."

I felt sure that the only way to break this deadlock was to eliminate John Watson from his continued dominance over the big gifts division. For the next meeting of our executive committee I prepared an elaborate plan for a revised campaign structure which would eliminate the big gifts division, as such, and thus eliminate Watson. We met at lunch on Friday. I explained my plan and was, I suspect, deviously diplomatic about it. Everyone saw through the scheme. Everyone was sorry for Watson. He had really worked very hard over the years, and was very proud of his relation with the big givers. The committee unanimously voted down my plan.

I returned to my office much disheartened. As long as Watson remained at the head of that division the Community Chest could not grow. Meanwhile the city was growing in size and wealth, and the big givers were becoming more wealthy. At the same time the financial needs of the social agencies and their clients were increasing, but could not be met. I determined to resign and seek work in some other community. Having written my resignation, I decided to show it first to Andrew Fraser. He was a new member of our executive committee. He had recently made a fortune. He was young, vigorous, and well-liked. Had my plan been approved, I had hoped he would head it up, in effect taking Watson's place and breaking the deadlock.

I went to Fraser's office and showed him my letter of resignation. He read it, reached for the phone and called the president of the Chest. (It was then Friday afternoon.) Fraser asked that a special meeting of the executive committee be called for Monday noon. At that meeting Fraser explained that he had a new plan for approaching the big givers during the next campaign. He then explained what the plan was. (It was substantially the same as the plan they had voted down on Friday.) It sounded better when he said it. The president asked him whether, if the plan were approved, he would be willing to head it up. Fraser said yes. It was unanimously approved, and Watson, seeing how things were going, even offered to give Fraser all the help he could. Under Fraser's leadership the deadlock was broken. Fraser increased his own gift and got increases from most of the big givers, and the campaign was successful in reaching a much higher goal. All because the right man presented the plan!

Zoning in a New England Town, U.S.A.

Many years ago the small New England town in which I live had no zoning ordinance. A property owner in the most desirable location in town, even adjoining the village green, could have sold to a buyer who wished to construct a gasoline filling station, and no one could have prevented it. The Men's Association became alarmed, and appointed a committee to study the need for zoning. Experts from New York were invited to come and speak to us on the subject. The committee prepared a report recommending a zoning ordinance to be presented to the Town Meeting for adoption. At the next monthly meeting of the Men's Association it was my duty, as chairman of the committee, to read the report and move its adoption. When I took my seat, Mr. Jamieson, a newcomer in town, rose to second the motion. He spoke at length until the members became restless. He had been in town only about four years, and was a New York commuter and a member of the Stock Exchange. He was somewhat pompous and overbearing in his manner, and distinctly unpopular. New York commuters were a minority, and were looked upon with disfavor by the old inhabitants. I, myself, had lived there only fifteen years. I should have arranged to have a "native" second my motion.

As Mr. Jamieson's harangue continued, I felt a pull at my coattail. Henry Murphy, one of our oldest and most honored citizens, leaned forward and whispered in my ear: "If that fellow doesn't sit down your motion is lost." Mr. Murphy had once been our postmaster. He and his relatives had lived in our town for generations, and he knew the temper of his neighbors. I rose abruptly and asked Mr. Jamieson if I might interrupt. "On second thought," I said, "I think we should think over this report carefully and vote on it at our next meeting. I therefore withdraw my motion." Mr. Jamieson, still on his feet, shouted: "If Mr. King is afraid to sponsor the motion, I'm not. I move we adopt it tonight." He looked about the room until at last he secured a half-hearted second to his motion. The question was put, and the motion

was overwhelmingly defeated. It was over two years before we could
secure the needed zoning ordinance. Probably the delay was due solely
to the fact that the wrong voice spoke in its favor.

To what extent do the principles we have been discussing apply on a national scale?

Here is an example which indicates that the same process can be
used successfully to influence the public's attitude nationally:

Vocational Rehabilitation in Israel

In 1955, the Minister of Labor in Israel appointed a committee to
consider the vocational rehabilitation and placement of handicapped
persons. The general attitude in the country at the time was that a
handicapped person could not be employed in normal industry, and
that such persons were fated either to live on public assistance or, if
fortunate, to be employed in a sheltered workshop. The only exception
to this applied to veterans of the War of Independence whose handicap
had resulted from war injury. They were covered by a law which
required every employer of more than 20 persons to employ handicapped war veterans to a minimum of 3 per cent of his total labor
force.

The committee met for a year under the chairmanship of the head
of the National Insurance Institute (a governmental agency similar to
the Social Security Administration in the United States). One of its
major recommendations was that a permanent council on vocational
rehabilitation be established to include representatives of all governmental and voluntary agencies concerned with the problem of the
handicapped person. An American agency working in the country in a
number of health and welfare areas was represented on the committee,
and its representative had urged the formation of a Council on Vocational Rehabilitation.

Recognizing the need for increasing the popular awareness of the
problem and of possible solutions to it, the American agency, which
was represented on the Council, proposed to the chairman that a
national conference on vocational rehabilitation be held which would

have as its purposes, first, to bring together all those with a direct or indirect concern with the problem, and second, by adequately publicizing the conference, to bring the subject to the attention of many people in the country. The American agency offered to provide part of the funds necessary for arranging and holding the conference, but it insisted that the local agencies, including the governmental departments, provide their share of the finances. It also offered to provide some staff time for the work involved in arranging the conference.

The chairman of the Council was interested, and agreed to have the proposal submitted to the next meeting of the Council. The representative of the American agency presented the proposal to the meeting of the Council, and it voted to call a national conference and to request the member agencies to participate in both its planning and its financing. A committee was appointed by the Council to arrange the conference, and the representative of the American agency was a member of the committee, while all the others represented local governmental and voluntary agencies.

The committee met for the first time in March and agreed that the conference be held in November or December that year. It was learned that Dr. Kessler, an outstanding American worker in the field of rehabilitation and president of the International Society for the Welfare of Cripples, would be in Australia in November, and after communicating with him the dates for the conference were set so that Dr. Kessler could return to the United States from Australia via Israel, and be a participant in the conference.

Subcommittees were appointed for such items as the arrangement of the program, printing of preliminary notification and invitations, preparing publicity material, arranging for meeting space, and various other mechanics involved in the conference.

As the preliminary work for the conference proceeded, more and more interest was manifested in it by manufacturers' and trade union groups who had previously not been very much interested in the problem. As a result, both the National Manufacturers Association and the Federation of Trade Unions designated representatives to the planning committee, and participated actively in the planning and financing of the conference. Both organizations printed a considerable amount of material in their own journals before the conference.

A preliminary announcement, together with a request for names of persons to be invited, was sent to a large number of organizations. The interest aroused by newspaper stories, by the articles, and by personal contact, resulted in a huge demand for invitations to the conference, and a formula had to be devised whereby the invitations were fairly distributed, but the number kept down.

Through the chairman of the council, it was possible to interest a number of governmental officials and cabinet ministers, and at one stage it was hoped that the President of the State himself would open the conference. This turned out to be impossible, but he did send a message to the conference which was read at the opening session by his Military Aide. The interest aroused was such that the opening session of the conference was attended by over 1,100 people (only 1,500 invitations had been issued). Among the speakers were the Ministers of Labor, Health, and Welfare, a representative of the Minister of Defense and the heads of the major voluntary agencies. The general session the following morning, and the group sessions in the morning and afternoon were attended by approximately 600 persons, and the general session which closed the conference the following evening was attended by some 500 persons.

Every newspaper in the country devoted a great deal of space to the conference and a number of them asked for feature articles which were used in the weeks that followed. The opening session of the conference was broadcast by the National Radio Station, and a special, previously taped program was broadcast the following week. In addition an interview with Dr. Kessler was broadcast a few evenings after the conference closed. In the month that followed the conference various papers presented were published in a number of trade and professional journals, and subsequently the bi-monthly journal of the Ministry of Welfare devoted a whole issue to papers presented at the conference. Incidentally, because Israelis are fanatical stamp collectors, arrangements were made with the post office for a special postmark to be used in Tel Aviv during the week of the conference, which urged the employment of handicapped persons. It had been hoped to have a special stamp issued, but that became too difficult to arrange.

While it is difficult to estimate the specific results of the conference, there is no doubt that public statements by cabinet members clearly involved some commitment by their departments and at least a recognition by those responsible for the Government that handicapped persons were entitled to a fair opportunity for employment. The Knesset, within a few months after the conference, passed the bill prohibiting discrimination against handicapped persons in labor exchanges, and even before the bill was passed, the labor exchange administrator established a special division for registration and placement of handicapped persons.[7]

How widely applicable are the principles we have been discussing?

In the early 1900's Booth Tarkington wrote a play called "The "Man from Home" asked where he learned such adroitness. The performs prodigious feats of shrewdness and diplomacy in a European city. The play, though ridiculed by dramatic critics, ran for years in the United States. It toured Europe and made the little town of Kokomo world famous. One line in the play will serve as a text for our discussion of the question above.

A European nobleman who became a friend and admirer of the "Man from Home" asked where he learned such adroitness. The "Man from Home" replied: "There are as many *kinds* of people in Kokomo as in Pekin." People are people, with similar needs and aspirations, wherever we may find them. Although they differ infinitely individually, they differ much less geographically. Because a majority of the case illustrations cited above have been drawn from Asia and Africa, do not assume that self-help and community action are not practiced in other parts of the world. Here is a case which I culled from a newspaper from Ireland:

Kilworth, Ireland

The function took place high above the village of Kilworth [Cork County]. Twelve months ago the people of the townlands of Kilally and Ballinrush had to draw their domestic water across the fields and then allow it to settle before it could be used. Yesterday they were able to turn on the taps in their own homes and see the product of their own work and co-operation.

It was the end of a gigantic "do-it-yourself" program by the people of that district, who, inspired by the Muintir na-tire spirit [a rural community organization started shortly after World War II by Father Hayes of County Tipperary which has now spread throughout Ireland] and a local dispensary doctor, gave their time, energy, and money, in seeing that a dream became reality. . . .

Dr. Sean O'Flynn, Chairman of the County Federation, Muintir na-tire, and of the local Guild [said] that the local people would not rest now that one phase had been achieved. They intended to go ahead with a sewerage scheme, and were already working in other parts of the parish on community water schemes of the type just opened.

. . . . .

The scheme, in which the water is pumped from the well on the site and gravity fed to the pipe-line system over a distance of four miles of countryside, was first considered 12 months ago, and plans were drawn up and approved by the Department [of local Government] . . . which made engineers available with technical knowledge. . . .

Teams of men and boys dug the trenches, installed sinks and taps, and laid five miles of Wavinpiping, all in their spare time. There were meetings and unending hard work for everybody, but now 30 homes have water at the rate of 30 gallons an hour. It took 6,000 man hours to see the scheme finished and the voluntary effort saved an estimated £1,200. The total cost of the scheme was about £3,500 excluding voluntary effort but with the Government grant of £50 per house and a similar amount from the County Council, the local contribution amounted to less than £17 per house, shared according to the ability to pay.

There are now five similar schemes going ahead in the Kilworth area to bring water to a further 150 homes.[8]

Neither should it be assumed that voluntary community action of this kind is an invention of the twentieth century. It has been practiced for centuries in many cultures in many parts of the world, although it is dying out in others. It was particularly prevalent in pioneer civilizations where one man could meet his needs only by the voluntary help of his neighbors. In the early settlements in the United States, log cabins were traditionally built by house-raising "bees" in which all the neighbors volunteered their services, and the affair was accompanied with feasting and jollification. More recently, when I was a boy on a Wisconsin farm, the "thrashing" of the grain was performed co-operatively. The engine and "thrashing" machine and a small crew moved from farm to farm, and all able-bodied men in the district worked from dawn to dark voluntarily. We helped "thrash" their wheat and then they helped us, and the women of the neighborhood co-operated in serving five great meals a day.

Apparently such co-operative labor was at one time traditional in parts of Africa, then began to die out, and now is being revived. Here is an illustration:

Kitoi, Kenya

In 1957 it was possible to post a community development officer to that district. He was a Kamba who had been born and bred in the district, and his salary was met from an American assistance fund.

He set about introducing the idea of *mwethya* [Traditional voluntary group work whereby neighbors helped each other to break new land, harvest crops, and build houses. It had to a great extent died out since those concerned could not afford the customary hospitality and festivities which concluded their efforts.] in a limited area near the Administrative Headquarters, and within a year it had extended throughout the entire district.

· · · · ·

It is common for as many as two or three hundred men and women to be employed at one time digging bench terraces and pits for coffee or banana trees, plastering houses or cleaning up compounds. On some occasions this resulted in a shortage of tools such as hoes and shovels. As a result, half of the people would be resting or singing to encourage those who were working. To remedy this state of affairs, tools have been issued on loan by the Location Council, and the work doubled. An interesting side-line to the problem of tools has been the establishment of field workshops where craftsmen are voluntarily employed in repairing implements as they get broken. This practical measure has been taken on the people's own initiative. . . .

It is an astounding sight to see hundreds of men and women all digging in unison to the accompaniment of a song. . . . In one area the people are making bricks for the construction of a hall, and for their own houses. In another, a pipe line nine miles long was completed in five weeks—a task which in the normal way would have taken five months. Tobacco-curing barns have been constructed, roads built, and dams excavated. It is not always, or even usually, conservatism and ignorance which is the main stumbling block to progress, but a failure to see how the necessary work can be achieved.

The Kitoi District is a good example of how the hardships and difficulties of merely providing the necessities of life hinder the introduction of measures to raise the standard of living. Take the case of manure. Most homesteads have a cattle enclosure in which a vast heap of valuable manure has accumulated. Much of this deteriorates and becomes useless through the baking of the sun. The construction of a cattle shed which would prevent this is often beyond the strength and means of most individuals, but group effort can overcome this obstacle and is now doing so daily.

The next problem is the transportation of these tons of manure to the fields to increase the yield of the crops. This again often defeats the individual, yet groups have often transported and spread as much as twenty tons in one day on the fields of the householders. Unless this manure is turned into the soil it is useless; the help of the group can achieve this before the sun's rays have had their destructive effect.

A fundamental principle of the work in this District is the fact that the organization of the groups rests with the people themselves and their chosen representatives. Their activities are not dictated by chiefs, headmen, or department staff. Such government officers are, however, there to give moral support and advice, and this is welcomed. The initiative as to where the group is to work on a particular day, what work it proposes to tackle, how the various members of the group are to be allocated, their duties, and so forth—all these rest with the group leaders. Thus at certain times of the year the most important task may be the preparation of the land for planting, at another it may be harvesting or winnowing. After the rains may be the best time for digging terraces, as the soil will be soft. Between the rains may be the best time for building dams. Thus, as in all agricultural communities, there is a reason for each activity, and during that time, side tracking to another may spell disaster. Only the people themselves are in a position to decide priorities, but all too often, government departments may have differing views as to what these priorities should be, and this may have unfortunate results unless the principles of community development are accepted.[9]

It might be assumed that so-called "well-developed" countries would have few unmet needs and hence less need for self-help community action. The reverse is the case. Appreciation of need grows with community education. The more sophisticated countries like England and the United States have the greatest number of voluntary citizens' organizations working to meet new needs. In the United States, rather than in England, there is one tendency, however, which gives me some concern. When a new function has been demonstrated under nongovernmental auspices (as was the case with the Woodhurst Mental Health Clinic) if the work is then assumed by the city government, the citizens who have the strongest interest in mental health may relax their efforts. Departmental heads are frequently lukewarm toward voluntary citizen co-operation with their work. The result may be perfunctory administration and a weakening of popular interest and financial interest. Not so in England. I recall that in Sheffield, for instance, of some 26 functions performed by the city government, every one had a citizens' committee, from the public health committee and the education committee to a committee in charge of the municipal graveyard. Each was a subcommittee of the large city council but on the recreation committee representatives of the Boy Scouts and Girl Guides were co-opted. On the educational committee sat representatives of privately supported schools, and so on. At the

City of East Ham I was invited to attend a meeting of the education committee. There were 40 members, and they were engaged in selecting a new principal for one of their schools. The education officer (superintendent of education) introduced each candidate for a brief interview. Then slips of paper were distributed. Each member voted, and the choice was made. Some may think that this method is carrying citizen participation too far, but it certainly must result in actively involving many volunteers in their government, thereby building a more active and well-informed citizenry.

There is some danger that in some of our cities in the United States the proper accent on efficient, professional administration is stressed without regard to the desirability of building a strong, informed citizenry by involving volunteer citizens wherever possible. In Sheffield I sat next to the chief public assistance officer (commissioner of public welfare) at the meeting of the City Council when final action was being taken on the next year's budget for all departments. He said nothing, and appeared relaxed and confident when his own departmental budget came up for discussion. Several strong speeches were made in its favor by citizens who were members of this public assistance committee. Members of the recreation committee and some other committees attacked it as too large, the Depression was still on, and the proposed budget would grant a big increase. I asked the public assistance officer when he was going to speak. He said, "Oh, I did my speaking last night." He meant that the evening before in a session of his public assistance committee he had briefed the members of his committee who were to speak at the public session of the City Council, and the whole strategy of supporting the proposed budget increase had been marked out. Speeches by volunteer community leaders would be more effective than a speech by the salaried executive. This proved to be true. The budget was adopted as requested. Obviously these community leaders, by taking part in this experience, became more competent to serve their city in the future.

As has been said above, the limit to felt needs is not actual but psychological, and expands as enlightenment increases. Community education grows with community action, and new needs come into view. This process, however, is by no means steady. After a spurt of community enthusiasm we may expect a period when the community lies fallow. At such times the community worker who has served as a catalyst may be transferred to another community which is less advanced, but ripe for stimulation.

The role of the *volunteer* community leader, however, is not over. If anything, his responsibility increases. It is for him to see that enthusiasm does not flag and that the cause is kept alive awaiting the right time to push actively ahead again. This is the period which will really test the skill of the *trained community worker* who has now passed on to other fields of activity. It is what *continues to happen* after he leaves that is the test of his ability to leave behind him volunteer community leaders stronger for his sojourn among them, and able to prevent the community from backsliding.

*   *   *

Summary. The trained community worker should not be above dirtying his hands in working *with* the people. He is not to pose as a superior doing something *for* them. He should beware of underestimating the role of women in community action, which may be as important as that of men, in any culture. The emotional urges of volunteer community leaders, which are sometimes destructive, can be tactfully redirected so as to be helpful in community action. Methods which work well in community action on a local scale can be equally useful nationally. It is frequently better for the trained community worker to arrange for a volunteer community leader to serve as a spokesman, than to speak himself. The principles that we have been discussing in this book apply in all cultures and all countries. They are not new but were probably practiced before the dawn of history.

APPENDIX

Concerning definitions

Mark Twain was allergic to punctuation marks. He considered omitting them entirely and placing an ample supply in an appendix. The reader could then select according to his taste and insert them where he wished.

I am allergic to definitions. I have seen many precious hours wasted in wrangling over the precise words to describe "community development" or "community organization," or the exact line to be drawn between these two processes. In this book I have endeavored to avoid this battle of semantics by choosing "community action" as a term to embrace both these embattled phrases. I have not defined community action with any exactness. In this book you will find some sixty-two cases which will illustrate what I mean better than any words I can choose to define it. When you are on a job engaged in community action, striving to the best of your ability, you will not need an academic definition, nor will one be of any help to you.

If you still have an appetite for definitions, here is an ample supply:

COMMUNITY DEVELOPMENT

1. A movement designed to promote better living for the whole community with the active participation [of], and if possible on the initiative of, the community, but if this initiative is not forthcoming

spontaneously, by the use of techniques for arousing and stimulating it in order to secure its active and enthusiastic response to the movement. (Study Conference at Hartwell House, Aylesbury, Buckinghamshire, Sept., 1957; Her Majesty's Stationery Office, London, 1958; p. 2.)

2. The processes by which the efforts of the people themselves are united with those of governmental authorities to improve the economic, social, and cultural conditions of communities, to integrate these communities into the life of the nation, and to enable them to contribute fully to national progress. It should not be regarded simply as a series of episodes embodied in concrete achievements; success in these, important though they may be, is less important than the qualitative changes expressed in attitudes and relationships, which add to human dignity, and increase the continuing capacity of the people to help themselves to achieve goals which they determine for themselves. (United Nations Economic and Social Council Document E/2931, 18 Oct., 1956)

3. A process of social action in which the people of a community organize themselves for planning and action; define their common and individual needs and problems; make group and individual plans to meet their needs and solve their problems; execute these plans with a maximum of reliance upon community resources; and supplement these resources when necessary with services and material from governmental and nongovernmental agencies outside the community. (ICA Manual Order No. 2710.1, July 2, 1957)

4. A process designed to create conditions of economic and social progress for the whole community with its active participation and the fullest possible reliance upon the community's initiative. (Social Progress Through Community Development, U. N. Bureau of Social Affairs, New York, 1955)

Community Organization

1. Community organization . . . has been defined as the process of bringing and maintaining a progressively more effective adjustment between social welfare resources and social welfare needs within a geographic area or functional field. Its goals are consistent with all social work goals in that its primary focus is upon needs of people and provision of means of meeting these needs in a manner consistent with the precepts of democratic living. (C. F. McNeil, "Community Organization for Social Welfare," *Social Work Year Book,* American Association of Social Workers, Inc., 1951.)

2. Community organization is the planned, co-operative effort to advance the over-all well-being of the community. (Dr. Irwin T. Saunders, University of Kentucky, 1953)

3. Community organization for social welfare is the process of bringing about and maintaining adjustment between social welfare needs and social welfare resources in a geographical area or a special field of service. (Arthur Dunham, *Community Welfare Organization Principles and Practices,* Thomas Y. Crowell Co., New York, 1958)

4. A process by which a community identifies its needs or objectives, develops the confidence and will to work at these needs or objectives, finds the resources (internal and/or external) to deal with these needs or objectives, takes action in respect to these and in so doing extends and develops co-operative and collaborative attitudes in the community. (Murray G. Ross, *Community Organization, Theory and Principles* (New York: Harper & Brothers, 1955).

Source Materials by Chapters

The case materials in this book come from a great variety of sources, including some incidents and situations that appeared in other books by the author, which are now out of print and unavailable for most students and teachers.

There are no references for Chapter I.

II

1. Clarence King, *Working with People in Small Communities* (New York: Harper & Brothers, 1959).
2. Quoted in Elting E. Morison, *Turmoil and Tradition* (Boston: Houghton Mifflin Co., 1960).
3. Najmeh Najafi, *Reveille for a Persian Village,* Helen Hinckley, ed. (New York: Harper & Brothers, 1958). Reprinted by permission of Harper & Row, Publishers, and by McIntosh and Otis, Inc. United States, Canada, and British Commonwealth, and Open Market rights are granted by the copyright owner.
4. Carl C. Taylor, "Making a Community Development Program Work," *Community Development Review,* International Co-operation Administration, Dec., 1958.
5. Charlotte Viall Wiser and William H. Wiser, *Behind Mud Walls* (New York: Friendship Press, 1946).
6. "Sarbandan," in *Reveille for a Persian Village (op. cit.,* Note 3 above).
7. William Foote Whyte, *Street Corner Society* (Chicago: University of Chicago Press, 1955). Copyright © 1955 by the University of Chicago.
8. *Behind Mud Walls (op. cit.,* Note 5 above).
9. "Ocampo," in *Working with People in Small Communities (op. cit.,* Note 1).
10. Conference with Roger Wolcott, International Co-operation Administration (ICA), Apr. 12, 1961.

III

1. Clarence King, *Working with People in Small Communities* (New York: Harper & Brothers, 1959).

2. From a personal letter from Mrs. Jean Ogden of the University of Virginia.
3. David S. Ritchie, "Work Camping in Africa," *The Friends Journal,* Nov. 1, 1960.
4. An office memorandum by William J. Cousins, ICA, Washington, D.C.
5. Conference with Dr. Katherine Holtzclaw, ICA, Apr. 12, 1961.
6. From "Program Newsletter" of Save-the-Children Federation, Norwalk, Conn. U.S.A., July 15, 1959. See also beginning of Chapter II above.
7. An office memorandum of Apr. 26, 1961, by William J. Cousins, ICA, Washington, D.C.
8. From *Progress Through Self-Help,* by T. G. Askwith, Commissioner for Community Development, Kenya (Nairobi, Kenya: East African Literature Bureau, 1960).

IV

1. Clarence King, *Organizing for Community Action* (New York: Harper & Brothers, 1948), OP (out of print).
2. Jacinta Muriel de García (assistant professor and field work supervisor, University of Puerto Rico School of Social Work) in Apr., 1961, issue of *Social Work,* journal of National Association of Social Workers, 95 Madison Ave., New York, N.Y., U.S.A. By permission.
3. *Organizing for Community Action* (*op. cit.,* Note 1 above).
4. An article in *The Family,* Nov., 1930, quoted in *Organizing for Community Action* (*op. cit.*) By permission of Family Service Association of America.
5. *Reveille for a Persian Village* (*op. cit.,* Note 3 in Chapter II above). Copyright © 1958 by Najmeh Najafi and Helen Hinckley Jones. Reprinted by permission of Harper & Row, Publishers.
6. *Organizing for Community Action* (*op. cit.,* Note 1 above).
7. From the 1952 "Report of the Division of Community Education," Department of Education, Puerto Rico.
8. Personal observation by the author.
9. Clarence King, *Working with People in Small Communities* (New York: Harper & Brothers, 1959).
10. Freeland Abbott, "The Makatab of Bahawalpur," Education Supplement, *Saturday Review,* New York, July 15, 1961. By permission.
11. "Report on U.S. Aid Education Projects," 1953-1957.
12. "The Story of Fundamental Education in Iran" by Luauna Bowles, 1960.

13. "Community School Education in Taiwan," ICA Mutual Security Mission in China, Tapei, Taiwan, July 1957.
14. *Community Education*, 50th Year Book of the National Society for the Study of Education (U.S.A.), p. 152.

V

1. Thor Heyerdahl, *Kon-Tiki: Across the Pacific*. Copyright 1950 by Thor Heyerdahl. Published in the U.S. by Rand McNally & Company, Chicago, Ill. By permission.
2. Personal observation by the author.
3. Regional Conference on Community Development at Teheran, Nov. 27-30, 1954.
4. Taken from the *Report of the Mission on Community Organization and Development in South and Southeast Asia*, United Nations, 1953.
5. *Ibid.*
6. *Ibid.*
7. Foreword to *Pilot Project, India*, by Albert Mayer (Berkeley, Calif.: University of California Press, 1959). By permission.
8. *Pilot Project, India* (*op. cit.*, Note 7 above). Memorandum in Apr., 1952, from Albert Mayer to Tarlok Singh, then Deputy Secretary of the National Planning Commission. By permission.
9. From "Report on Near East Foundation Program of Rural Development in Varamin Plains of Iran, 1946-1959."
10. Conference with Roger Wolcott of ICA, in Washington, D.C., Apr. 12, 1953.

VI

1. Clarence King, *Your Committee in Community Action* (New York: Harper & Brothers, 1950), OP.
2. A. Houttuyn Pieper, "Community Organization in the North Veluwe" (The Netherlands), International Review of Community Development (Rome, 1958). By permission of the author.
3. From a term paper of one of my students.
4. Elizabeth Gray Vining, *Friend of Life* (Philadelphia: J. B. Lippincott Company, 1958). By permission.
5. South Pacific Commission, *Social Development Notes for 1952*, No. 9.
6. *Organizing for Community Action* (*op. cit.*, Note 1 in Chapter IV), OP.

VII

1. Morris Eisenstein, "Some Problems in Neighborhood Organization," an unpublished address.

2. B. Chatterjee and Marshall B. Clinard, *Organizing Citizens' Development Councils* (Delhi: Delhi Municipal Council, Department of Urban Community Development, 1961). By permission.
3. Recorded interview with Hope Murrow prepared for discussion at Alumni Conference, New York School of Social Work, May, 1961.
4. Stanley B. Winters, "New Challenges to Neighborhoods," in *The Crisis*, Feb., 1961. By permission.
5. *The Management of Neighborhood Change*, Chicago Commission on Human Relations, 1959.
6. Kalervo Oberg, *Chonin de Cima, A Rural Community in Minas Gervais, Brazil* (published by U.S./O.M., Brazil).
7. *Behind Mud Walls* (*op. cit.*, Note 5 in Chapter II).

VIII

1. Letter from J. D. Mezirow of the Institute of International Studies, University of California at Berkeley, Calif., Sept. 28, 1960.

IX

1. Dalip S. Saund, *Congressman from India* (New York: E. P. Dutton & Co., Inc., 1960). Permission covers world rights in the English language.
2. Report of American Friends Service Committee on "Social and Technical Assistance in India," Dec. 31, 1956.
3. Conference with Dr. Katherine Holtzclaw, ICA, Washington, D.C.
4. *Human Problems in Technological Change*, Edward H. Spicer, ed. (New York: Russell Sage Foundation, 1952). By permission.
5. Dr. Katherine Holtzclaw (see Note 3 above).
6. *Organizing for Community Action* (*op. cit.* in Note 1, Chapter IV).
7. Memorandum given me by Aubrey Mallach.
8. From the *Cork Weekly Examiner*, May 25, 1961. By permission of the editor.
9. From *Progress Through Self-Help*, by T. G. Askwith, Commissioner for Community Development, Kenya (Nairobi, Kenya: East African Literature Bureau, 1960).